THE
ENGLISH
CASTLES
ALMANAC

Published in association with the English Tourist Board

Lochar Publishing • Moffat • Scotland

© Lochar Publishing, 1992.

Published by Lochar Publishing Ltd,
Moffat, Scotland DG10 9ED.

A catalogue record for this book is available from the British Library.

ISBN 1-874027-35-6.

Typeset in Times 8pt on 9pt by Origination and printed by Cambus in Scotland.

The information contained in this guide has been published in good faith and every effort has been made to ensure its accuracy. Neither Lochar Publishing Ltd nor the English Tourist Board can accept any responsibility for error or misinterpretation. All liability for loss, disappointment, negligence or other damage caused by reliance on the information contained in this publication, or in the event of bankruptcy or liquidation or cessation of the trade of any company, individual or firm mentioned is hereby excluded.

INTRODUCTION

Castles are an integral part of England's heritage and throughout the country you will discover a wealth of places to explore. Some have changed very little from the time they were built; others are still family homes having been added to over the generations; all provide an insight into the history and heritage of England. Even where the original buildings have fallen into ruin, the surviving remains can evoke an impression of what castle life must have been like all those centuries ago. No two English castles are the same and many were built on spectacular sites commanding panoramic views of the surrounding countryside.

This guide contains a selection of some of the best known locations open to the public across the country. The castles featured range from examples of early Norman motte and bailey sites, through later, more sophisticated concentric castles to crenellated manor houses. All provide fascinating days out for adults and children alike.

Each individual entry is illustrated in colour and provides all the practical information you need to plan and enjoy your visit. A concise description mentions the castle's history and any special features. Up-to-date information is given on location, opening times, admission charges, facilities and accessibility for disabled visitors.

Every effort has been made to ensure that the information given is correct; however, details can change. Please check before setting out, especially if you have any special requirements.

GLOSSARY

BAILEY   Enclosed defensive courtyard

BARBICAN   Outer tower, part of defense of main gateway

BASTION   Defensive projection from main walls; either platform or small tower

BATTER   Inclined face of wall

BATTLEMENTS   Parapet consisting of stone *merlons* interspersed with *embrasures*

BUTTRESS   Projection from wall for additional support

CONCENTRIC CASTLE   Castle with two or more enclosing walls. The innermost being higher than the outer

CRENELLATE   To add *battlements*. 'Licence to crenellate' meant royal permission to fortify a manor house

CURTAIN WALL   Outer wall often incorporating defensive towers

DONJON   Original name for the *keep* or main tower. Prisoners were often kept in the lowest part, hence dungeons

DRAWBRIDGE   Wooden bridge across the moat that could be raised or lowered

EMBRASURE   Small, splayed opening between *merlons* in outer wall or *battlements*

FOSSE   A ditch

GARDEROBE   Latrine, usually in outer wall

KEEP   Main tower

LANCET   Long narrow window with pointed head

LINEAR CASTLE   Castle with *baileys* or enclosed courtyards arranged in a chain

MACHIOLATION   Stone platform built out from *battlements* with holes through which missiles could be dropped

MERLON   Stone part of *battlements*, often pierced with arrow slits

MOAT   Ditch surrounding castle, usually water-filled

MOTTE   A natural or artificial mound, on which a *donjon* or *keep* was built

MURDER HOLE   Opening in gatehouse ceiling or wall through which defenders could attack the enemy

NEWEL   Centre-post of winding staircase

OUBLIETTE   Dungeon where prisoners were left to starve to death

PELE TOWER   Tower stronghold without outer defensive walls

PORTCULLIS   Heavy wooden and iron grille suspended in grooves which could be dropped to block a gateway

POSTERN   Back exit from castle, often used for escape

RAMPART   Defensive stone or earth wall surrounding castle

SLIGHT   Damage or demolish castle to make it indefensible

SOLAR   Upper-level withdrawing room used by the lord and his family and guests

WARD   Enclosed defensive courtyard

ACTON BURNELL CASTLE

Acton Burnell, Near Shrewsbury, Shropshire.

Ownership: English Heritage.

Status: English Heritage.

General Description: A warm sandstone shell of a fortified thirteenth-century manor house. Acton Burnell is one of the most intact fortified manor houses in England. It owes its second name to Roger Burnell, a favourite clerical civil servant of Edward I who became first Chancellor of England and later Bishop of Bath and Wells. The manor was granted to Burnell in 1284 by Edward I with a lucrative permission to cut timber in the royal forests of Shropshire. The house was completed in 1293 and remained in the Burnell's family until it was abandoned in 1420.

Open: Any reasonable time.

Admission: None – free site.

Facilities: Parking only.

Disabled Access: Yes – access only.

Additional Information: Picnics in grounds, dogs on lead.

ALNWICK CASTLE

Estates Office, Alnwick Castle, Alnwick, Northumberland, NE66 1NQ.
(0665) 510777

Ownership: Duke of Northumberland.

Status: Historic Houses Association.

General Description: This magnificent border fortress dates
back to the eleventh-century, when the earliest parts of the
present castle were erected by Yvo de Vescy, the first Norman
Baron of Alnwick, who became the owner of the town soon
after 1096. The Percy family, who had accompanied William
the Conqueror in 1066, came into ownership in 1309. The
main restoration work bringing the castle to its present appearance, was carried out by the 4th Duke between 1854 and
1865. The rugged medieval exterior belies the richness of the
interior, decorated in the classical style of the Italian
Renaissance: this replaced the Gothic decoration carried out
by Robert Adam in the eighteenth-century. The principal
apartments including the Armoury, Guard Chamber and
Library are on view, also the Dungeon, Stage Coach, and
museum of early British and Roman relics. There are pictures
by Titian, Canaletto, Van Dyck and other famous artists,
together with fine furniture, Messian China and various
historical heirlooms.

Open: 16th April to 10th October, 11 a.m. – 5 p.m.

Admission: Adults: £3; Senior Citizens: £2.60; Children: £2;
Family Ticket: £8.

Facilities: Free parking, gift shop.

Disabled Access: No.

Additional Information: No dogs, no picnics.

ARUNDEL CASTLE

Arundel Castle, West Sussex, BN18 9AB.
(0903) 883136

Ownership: Arundel Castle Trustees Limited.

Status: Independent Charitable Trust.

General Description: This great castle, home of the Dukes of
Norfolk, dates from the Norman Conquest. Containing a very
fine collection of furniture and paintings Arundel Castle is
still the family home, reflecting the changes of nearly a
thousand years. Personal possessions of Mary Queen of Scots
and a selection of historical, religious and heraldic items from
the Duke of Norfolk's collection are also on display. The Duke
of Norfolk is the Premier Duke, the title having been
conferred on Sir John Howard in 1483 by his friend King
Richard III. The Dukedom also carries with it the hereditary
office of Earl Marshal of England. Among the historically
famous members of the Howard family are Lord Howard of
Effingham who with Drake repelled the Spanish Armada; the
Earl of Surrey, the Tudor poet and courtier and the 3rd Duke
of Norfolk, uncle of Anne Boleyn and Catherine Howard both
of whom became wives of King Henry VIII.

Open: 1st April to 30th October, Sundays to Fridays inclusive
from 12 p.m. – 5 p.m. Last admission on any day is 4 p.m.
The Castle is not open on Saturdays.

Admission: Adults: £3.60; Senior Citizens: £3.10; Children
(aged 5-15): £2.60; Group Rate (twenty or more): Adults:
£3.10; Senior Citizens: £2.90; Children: £2.30.

Facilities: The restaurant serves home made food for lunch and afternoon tea, pre-booked parties are welcome and menus are available on request. The shop offers items chosen by the Countess of Arundel. Parking for 200 cars within the Castle grounds. Council Coach and Car Park opposite the Castle entrance.

Disabled Access: As most of the public rooms are on the first floor, wheelchair visitors should enter via a special door with a bell-pull. An attendant will escort the visitor to the lift where he/she will transfer to the Castle's wheelchair which just fits the lift. Adapted toilets within the Castle and at the Tea Garden.

Additional Information: No special provision for picnics. Dogs are NOT admitted.

ASHBY DE LA ZOUCH CASTLE

South Street, Ashby De La Zouch, Leicestershire, LE6 5PR.
(0503) 413343

Status: English Heritage.

General Description: The impressive ruins of this Norman castle are dominated by the magnificent Hastings Tower. The tower still stands over 80 feet high, rising vertically from the neat, manicured lawns that now surround the castle. Evidence of a turbulent history is all around. The tower was literally split in two during the Civil War, when the castle played an important role in the Royalist defence of the Midlands. In more peaceful times, Walter Scott rescued Ashby De La Zouch from obscurity. He set a number of pageant scenes from his famous book *Ivanhoe* at the castle.

Open: Good Friday or 1st April (whichever is earlier) to 30th September, daily, 10 a.m. – 6 p.m., 1st October to Maundy Thursday or 31st March (whichever is earlier), Tuesday to Sunday, 10 a.m. – 4 p.m.

Admission: Adults: 95p; Senior Citizens, Students & UB40 holders: 75p; Children: 45p; special party rates.

Facilities: Car park, refreshments nearby, underground passage (bring a torch!), access for disabled (grounds only).

Disabled Access: Access to grounds.

AYDON CASTLE

Aydon Castle, Corbridge, Northumberland, NE45 5JP.
(0434) 632450

Status: English Heritage.

General Description: One of the finest fortified manor houses in England, dating from the late thirteenth century and situated in a position of great natural beauty. Its survival, remarkably intact, can be attributed to it's conversion to a farm house in the seventeenth century.

Open: April to September, daily, 10 a.m. – 6 p.m.

Admission: Adult: £1.50; Concession: £1.10; Child: 75p.

Facilities: Parking, refreshments available.

Disabled Access: Wheelchair access to ground floor.

Additional Information: Shop, toilets, suitable for picnics, dogs allowed in some areas.

BARNARD CASTLE

Castle House, Barnard Castle, Co. Durham, DL12 9AT.
(0833) 38212

Status: English Heritage.

General Description: Barnard Castle is a ruined Norman Castle, built by the Baliol family in the twelfth century. The castle is divided into four wards, the Town Ward, Outer Ward, Middle Ward and Inner Ward. A total area of six and a half acres, the castle stands high above the River Tees with magnificent views from the Round Tower of the river and upper Teesdale. It was left to ruin in 1630 by Sir Henry Vane, who stripped it of its lead glass and wood to help with the building work at Raby Castle.

Open: Summer season: 1st April to 30th September, 7 day week, 10 a.m. – 6 p.m. Winter season: 1st October to 31st March, 6 days week, 10 a.m. – 4 p.m. closed on Mondays.

Admission: Adults: £1.10; Senior Citizens, Students and UB40 holders: 85p; Children: 55p.

Facilities: Parking in town 200 yards.

Disabled Access: Access yes, facilities no.

Additional Information: Dogs and picnics are allowed.

BEESTON CASTLE

Beeston, Tarporley, Cheshire, CW6 9TX.
(0829) 260464

Status: English Heritage.

General Description: Standing majestically on sheer, rocky crags which fall sharply away from the castle walls, Beeston has possibly the most stunning views of the surrounding countryside of any castle in England and a history stretching back over 2,500 years.

Open: April to September, daily, 10 a.m. – 6 p.m.
October to March, Tuesday to Sundays, 10 a.m. – 4 p.m.

Admission: Adult: £1.80; Concession: £1.40; Child: 90p.

Facilities: Parking.

Additional Information: Toilets, guidebook, dogs allowed in some areas.

BELVOIR CASTLE

Belvoir, Grantham, Lincs.
(0476) 870262

Ownership: Duke of Rutland.

Status: Historic Houses Association.

General Description: Belvoir Castle commands a magnificent view over the surrounding countryside. The name, Belvoir, meaning beautiful view, dates back to Norman times, when Robert de Todeni, Standard Bearer to William the Conqueror, built the first Castle on this superb site. Destruction caused by two Civil Wars (in the fifteenth and seventeenth centuries) and by a catastrophic fire in 1816 have breached the continuity of Belvoir's history. The present building owes much to the inspiration and taste of Elizabeth, 5th Duchess of Rutland, and was built after the fire. Inside the Castle are notable art treasures, including works by Poussin, Holbein, Rubens and Reynolds; Gobelin and Mortlake tapestries; Chinese silks; furniture; fine porcelain and sculpture.

Open: 1st April to 1st October 1992; Tuesdays, Wednesdays, Thursdays, Saturdays, Sundays, Good Friday and Bank Holiday Mondays. Sundays only in October.
Open 11 a.m. – 5 p.m.

Admission: Adults: £3.20; Child (5-16 inclusive.): £2.20; Senior Citizens: £2.20. Party rate: Adults: £2.50; Schools/Youth groups: £1.80.

Facilities: Free car and coach parking, restaurant facilities within Castle, adventure play area, nature trail; special events most Sundays and Bank Holiday Mondays throughout the season including Medieval Jousting Tournaments.

Disabled Access: Parking for disabled available immediately adjacent to Castle, Toilet facilities at car park; ground floor only accessible to wheelchairs (restaurant situated on ground floor).

Additional Information: Picnic area, with tables, at car park. No dogs excepting guide dogs.

BERKELEY CASTLE

Berkeley, Gloucestershire, GL13 9BQ.
(0453) 810 332

Ownership: Mr John Berkeley.

Status: Historic Houses Association.

General Description: Berkeley Castle was completed in 1153 at the command of Henry II. Ever since it has been the home of the Berkeley family, one of England's oldest families. Twenty-four generations have gradually transformed a savage Norman fortress into a truly stately home full of treasures. Paintings by primarily English and Dutch masters, tapestries, furniture of an interesting diversity, silver and porcelain. Wander at leisure or join one of the free one-hour guided tours covering highlights such as the massive Keep with the Dungeon and the cell where King Edward II was murdered in 1327, the medieval buttery and kitchens, the historic Great Hall and the magnificent State Apartments. The Castle is surrounded by terraced Elizabethan Gardens and sweeping lawns. The Butterfly Farm is a tranquil oasis with hundreds of exotic butterflies in free flight.

Open: April: Tuesday to Sunday, 2 p.m. – 5 p.m. May to September: Tuesday to Saturday, 11 a.m. – 5 p.m & Sunday, 2 p.m. – 5 p.m. Bank Holiday Mondays, 11 a.m. – 5 p.m. October: Sundays only, 2 p.m. – 4.30 p.m.

Admission: Adult: £3.40; Child: £1.60; OAP/Student: £2.50. Groups of twenty-five or more: Adult: £3.00; Child: £1.50; OAP/Student: £2.50. Gardens only: Adult: £1; Child: 50p.

Facilities: Free car park and coach car park. Tea room (also serving light lunches), gift shop. Butterfly Farm, Admission: Adults: 50p; Child/OAP: 20p.

Disabled Access: Very limited access for disabled.

Additional Information: Large picnic lawn adjacent to car park. Dogs not admitted beyond car park.

<u>Berry Pomeroy Castle</u>

Berry Pomeroy, Totnes, Devon, TQ9 6LJ.
(0803) 866618

Ownership: Duke of Somerset.

Status: English Heritage.

General Description: Whether or not Berry Pomeroy can live up to its reputation of being the most haunted castle in Devon, it is certainly one of the most romantic. Set halfway up a wooded hillside, looking out over a deep ravine with a stream, it is an ideal site for a picnic – situated well away from the road and very serene and peaceful. Berry Pomeroy is unusual because it combines the remains of a fortified castle with those of a flamboyant courtier's mansion. The ruins of the fifteenth-century castle, built by the Pomeroy family, make an impressive sight. Built within the castle walls after being sold to the Seymour family, the mansion displays evidence of considerable splendour and a grand lifestyle.

Open: Good Friday or 1st April (whichever is earlier) to 30th September, daily, 10 a.m. – 6 p.m.

Admission: Adults: £1.50; Senior Citizens/Student Cards/UB40 Cards: £1.10; Child (under 16): 75p, Under 5 years: free. Special party rates.

Facilities: Free car park, toilets, refreshments and shop nearby. Site exhibition.

Disabled Access: Limited access to grounds and ground floor.

Additional Information: Dogs not admitted.

BICKLEIGH CASTLE

Bickleigh, Tiverton, Devon, EX16 8RP.
(0884) 855363

Ownership: Mr Noel Boxall.

Status: Privately owned.

General Description: Bickleigh Castle, a Royalist
stronghold and former home of the heirs of the Earls of
Devon and subsequently of the Carew family, lies on the
bank of the River Exe – an area of outstanding beauty. It has
all the attractions of a lived-in home yet features over 900
years of history and architecture. The eleventh-century
detached Chapel is the oldest complete building in Devon and
the Gatehouse, with its Armoury and Guard Room, features
Cromwellian arms and armour and fine Tudor furniture and
oil paintings. The most imposing room in the Castle is the
Great Hall with its minstrel's gallery. The 'Tudor' bedroom
includes an ornately carved large four-poster bed, and the
only known copy of a Cluny tapestry. After the besiege of the
Castle in the Civil War Sir Henry Carew replaced a portion of
the fortified part by the farmhouse wing and visitors see the
family Dining Room, Sitting Room, and the Garden Room
with its impressive stone carved overmantel. Outside the
original moat is now a colourful water garden and the
enormous Mound is covered in virtually every variety of
rhododendron. In addition visitors see the Museum of
eighteenth- to twentieth-century domestic objects and toys:
children are welcome to ride the period Rocking Horses, the
maritime *Mary Rose* and *Titanic* exhibitions each have
Bickleigh connections and there are the World War II spy

and escape gadgets – the most complete collection in the UK.

Open: Easter week (Good Friday to Friday) and then Wednesdays, Sundays and Bank Holidays to late Spring Bank Holiday; then to early October daily (except Saturdays). All 2 p.m. – 5.30 p.m. Parties of twenty and over by prior arrangement at reduced rates.

Admission: Adults: £2.80; Children (5-15): £1.40; No reduction for Senior Citizens; 'Family' Tickets; Groups (minimum of twenty); £2.30.

Facilities: Large free Coach/Car Park, tearooms, Souvenir Shops.

Disabled Access: Normally ground floor only both of Castle and Museum/*Mary Rose*/Spy and Escape.

Additional Information: Picnic area with benches etc in Chapel orchard alongside the river. Dogs not allowed.

BODIAM CASTLE

Bodiam, Robertsbridge, East Street, TN32 5UA.
(0580) 830436

Ownership: The National Trust.

Status: The National Trust.

General Description: Bodiam Castle was built by Royal Licence of October 1385 'for the defence of the adjacent country and the resistance to our (The King's) enemies.' Destined never to stand siege, dismantled in the seventeenth century, Bodiam nevertheless remains the outstanding example of Medieval Military Architecture. It incorporated the latest military design features of the day but at the same time was a well appointed mansion for its builder Sir Edward Dalyngrigge. The virtual completeness of the exterior makes it a picturebook castle, and children enjoy the adventure of discovering every nook and cranny, not to mention the spiral staircases and battlements. Although a ruin, the floors have been replaced in some of the towers, and it is possible to go right to the top and enjoy impressive views of the surrounding countryside. In one of the towers, there is an audio visual display about life in a medieval castle and in another, a video showing how a knight was armed. A museum is situated next to the ticket office.

Open: Daily, 10 a.m. – 5.30 p.m. or sunset if earlier. Closed Sundays from November to March. Closed for Christmas.

Admission: Adult: £2.00; Child: £1.00; Parties of 20 or more by arrangement.

Facilities: Parking with shop and tearoom. Audio visual show inside the castle. Two education rooms with many hands on resources (pre-booking essential).

Disabled Access: WC for use of disabled.

Additional Information: Picnics in grounds. No dogs or picnics inside the castle.

BOLTON CASTLE

Leyburn, North Yorkshire, DL8 4ET.
(0969) 23981

Ownership: Private (H.A.N. Orde-Polilett)

General Description: Bolton Castle was built in the
fourteenth century by Richard Scrope. Bolton is an
impressive fortified manor house, one of the most complete
and original medieval dwellings in Yorkshire. The Scrope
family are mentioned in three of Shakespeare's plays
(*Richard II, Henry IV* and *Henry V*). Henry VI took refuge
there after losing the battle of Hexham. Mary Queen of Scots
was imprisoned there for six months. The castle is sparsely
furnished and very atmospheric!

Open: March to October, daily, 10 a.m. – 5 p.m.

Admission: Adult: £2.50; Child/Senior Citizens: £1.50.

Facilities: Parking, tea-room, shop.

Disabled Access: Nil.

Additional Information: Dogs not allowed.

BROUGH CASTLE

High Street, Brough, Kirby Stephen, Cumbria, CA17 4EJ.
(0930) 4219

Status: English Heritage.

General Description: Perched on a superb vantage point overlooking an old trade route, now the A66, this ancient site dates back to Roman times, the twelfth-century keep replaces an earlier stronghold destroyed by the Scots in 1174. The castle was restored by Lady Ann Clifford in the seventeenth century.

Open: April to September, daily, 10 a.m. – 6 p.m.
October to March, Tuesday to Sunday, 10 a.m. – 4 p.m.

Admission: Adult: 75p; Concession: 55p; Child: 40p.

Additional Information: Dogs allowed.

BROUGHAM CASTLE

Brougham, Penrith, Cumbria, CA10 2AA.
(0768) 62488

Ownership: English Heritage.

General Description: These impressive ruins on the banks of the River Eamont include an early thirteenth-century keep and water buildings. You can climb to the top of the keep and survey the domain of its eccentric one time owner Lady Anne Clifford, who restored the castle in the seventeenth century. There is a small exhibition of Roman tombstones from the nearby fort.

Open: All year: 1st April to 30th September, 10 a.m. – 6 p.m.; 1st October to 31st March, 10 a.m. – 4 p.m., closed Mondays, also closed Christmas Eve, Christmas Day, Boxing Day and New Years Day.

Admission: Adult: £1.10; Concession: 85p; Child: 55p.

Facilities: Parking available.

Disabled Access: To ground floor only – cobbled courtyard and entrance.

Additional Information: Dogs on lead, picnic by river.

BROUGHTON CASTLE

Broughton Castle, Banbury, Oxon, OX15 5EB.
(0295) 262624

Ownership: Lord Saye & Sele.

Status: Privately owned.

General Description: The castle, built in 1300 and greatly enlarged in 1550, is surrounded by a three acre moat and stands on a three acre island. It has been in the ownership of the family for over 600 years. Fine panelling and plasterwork of the sixteenth century. The castle was a meeting place for the Parliamentary leaders before the Civil War: besieged and captured after the battle of Edgehill in 1642.

Open: 20th May to 13th September, Wednesdays and Sundays also Thursdays in July and August and Bank Holiday Sundays and Bank Holiday Mondays (including Easter).

Admission: Adults: £2.80; Senior Citizens/Students: £2.10; Children: £1.40.

Facilities: Car park, tearoom, shop.

Disabled Access: Reasonably good – all ground floor.

Additional Information: Picnics in the park, dogs allowed in park and garden.

CAISTER CASTLE

West Caister, Near Gt. Yarmouth, Norfolk.
(057) 284-251

Ownership: Dr. P. R. Hill.

General Description: One of the last castles built in England – built more for comfort than defence by Sir John Fastolfe, K.G., P.C., in 1432 with £6,000 ransome money that he obtained from the Duke of Alencon. It took the place of a fortified Manor House built in the thirteenth century, the perimeter walls of which were equipped with arrow slits, and also gun ports. In the grounds is a fine purpose built building housing a very large number of antique cars.

Open: Mid May to last Friday in September, open every day except Sundays.

Facilities: Parking and tearoom.

Disabled Access: Yes.

Additional Information: Provision for picnics in castle grounds, dogs admitted on lead in grounds only.

CALSHOT CASTLE

Calshot, Hants, S04 1BR.
(0703) 892023

Status: English Heritage.

General Description: Henry VIII built this coastal fort in an excellent position, commanding the sea passage to Southampton. The fort houses an exhibition and re-created pre-World War I barrack room.

Open: 1st April to 30th September. Open daily 10 a.m. – 6 p.m.

Admission: Adults: £1.10; Senior Citizens, Unemployed (on production of UB40)/Students (with Student Card): 85p; Children (under 16): 55p (under 5's free).

Facilities: Parking, toilets.

Additional Information: No dogs allowed.

CARISBROOKE CASTLE

Carisbrooke, Newport, Isle of Wight, PO30 1XY.
(0983) 523107

Ownership: English Heritage.

Status: English Heritage.

General Description: For children, and not a few adults, Carisbrooke's main attraction today are the donkeys which work a sixteenth-century donkey wheel to pull water from the 161 foot deep well. There are seven acres of castle and earthworks to explore. You will find evidence of the castle's eleventh century origins, and of the sixteenth century modernisation which includes some of the finest surviving artillery defences. Most striking is the impressive gatehouse set into the walls, through which the visitor must pass to enter the castle. Walk along the ramparts, climb to the top of the shell keep and you will obtain splendid views of the castle and surrounding countryside. Charles I was imprisoned here in 1647/48 and on trying to escape, became wedged between the bars of a window.

Open: 1st April to 30th September, daily, 10 a.m. – 6 p.m. 1st October to 31st March, daily, 10 a.m. – 4 p.m.

Admission: Adults: £3.00; Senior Citizens/Students/UB40 holders: £2.30; Children: £1.50.

Facilities: On site parking free, cafeteria (Summer only), toilets.

Disabled Access: Access to ground floor for wheelchairs.

Additional Information: Picnic areas outside castle walls, dogs allowed.

CARLISLE CASTLE

Carlisle, Cumbria, CA3 8UR.
(0228) 31777

Status: English Heritage.

General Description: Impressive medieval castle, where Mary Queen of Scots was once imprisoned. A long tortuous history of warfare, struggling and family feuds. A real port cullis hangs menacingly in the gatehouse, there is a maze of passages and chambers, endless staircases to lofty towers and you can walk the high ramparts for stunning views. There is also a medieval manor house in miniature, a suite of medieval rooms refurnished as they might have been when used by the castle's former inhabitants. The museum of the King's Own Border Regiment is also in the castle.

Open: All year except Christmas Eve, Christmas Day, Boxing Day and New Years Day. 1st April to 30th September, 10 a.m. – 6 p.m. 1st October to 31st March, 10 a.m. – 4 p.m.

Admission: Adults: £1.80; Concessions: £1.40; Children: 90p.

Facilities: Parking either side of castle, toilets.

Disabled Access: To ground floor only.

Additional Information: Dogs allowed on lead, large lawned area outside castle.

CASTLE DROGO

Drewsteignton, Exeter, EX6 6PB.
(0647) 433306

Ownership: The National Trust.

Status: The National Trust.

General Description: Perched on a crag overlooking the Teign Gorge at 900 feet above sea-level, the castle is a marvel of the ingenuity of the architect Sir Edwin Lutyens. It was built between 1910 and 1930 and contains much to fascinate the family, magnificent craftsmanship in wood and granite, combining the grim splendours of a medieval fortress with the opulent luxuries required by the Drewe family, including its own hydroelectric and telephone systems. There are magnificent views of the wooded gorge of the Teign to Dartmoor beyond. Beautiful secluded garden also by Lutyens. Attractive walks through the surrounding spectacular countryside.

Open: 1st April to 1st November, 11 a.m. – 5.30 p.m. (last admission 5 p.m.).

Admission: Castle and grounds: £4.40. Grounds only: £2.00; Children 5-16 years: half price.

Facilities: Car park, counter service tearoom, waitress service restaurant, shop, croquet lawn with equipment for hire.

Disabled Access: Limit access to castle, access to garden restaurant etc., lavatory for disabled persons at visitor reception.

Additional Information: No dogs in castle or immediate surroundings.

CLIFFORD'S TOWER

Tower Street, York, YO1 2ED.
(0904) 646940

Status: English Heritage.

General Description: A thirteenth-century tower on one of two mottes thrown up by William the Conqueror to hold York. There are panoramic views of the city from the top of the tower.

Open: April to September, daily, 10 a.m. – 6 p.m., October to March, daily, 10 a.m. – 4 p.m.

Admission: Adults: £1.10; Concessions: 85p; Children: 55p; English Heritage members free.

Facilities: Parking.

COMPTON CASTLE

Compton, Near Paignton, South Devon.
(0803) 872112

Ownership: National Trust.

Status: National Trust.

General Description: Fortified manor house built in three stages 1340, 1450, 1520. Home of Sir Humphrey Gilbert, (who colonised Newfoundland in 1583). The Great Hall, Chapel, Solar, Old Kitchen, and Rose Garden are open. The Gilbert family are still in residence.

Open: 1st April to end October, Mondays, Wednesdays and Thursdays only, 10 a.m. – 12.15 p.m., 2 p.m. – 5 p.m. Last admission half hour before closing.

Admission: Adults: £2.40; Children: £1.20; Party rate: Adults: £1.80; Children: 90p.

Facilities: Car parking on grass, coach parking at Castle Barton opposite, restaurant at Castle Barton opposite main gate.

Disabled Access: Limited access for disabled visitors.

Additional Information: Dogs not allowed, picnics allowed in car park.

CONISBOROUGH CASTLE

Conisborough, Doncaster, South Yorkshire, DN12 3BU.
(0709) 863329

Status: English Heritage and Ivanhoe Trust.

General Description: The spectacular white circular keep of this twelfth-century castle rises above the River Don. It is the oldest circular keep in England and one of the finest medieval buildings. It houses a visitor centre and exhibition.

Open: April to September, daily, 10 a.m. – 6 p.m.
October to March, daily, 10 a.m. – 4 p.m.

Admission: Adults: £1.50; Concessions: £1.10; Children: 75p.

Facilities: Car park.

Disabled Access: Limited access.

CORFE CASTLE

Wareham, Dorset, BH20 SE2.
(0929) 480921

Ownership: National Trust.

Status: National Trust.

General Description: One of the most impressive ruins in England; former royal castle, besieged and slighted by parliamentary forces in 1646.

Open: 9th February to end October, daily, 10 a.m. – 5.30 p.m. or dusk if earlier. November to February, Saturday and Sunday only, 12 – 3.30 p.m.

Admission: Adults: £2.50; Children: £1.30; Parties: £2.00.

Facilities: National Trust shop, licensed restaurant serving lunch, coffee and cream teas.

Additional Information: Dogs on leads only.

CROFT CASTLE

Leominster, Hereford and Worcester, HR6 9PW.
(0568) 85 246

Ownership: The National Trust.

Status: The National Trust.

General Description: The four round corner towers and ancient walls date from the fourteenth or fifteenth century; inside, the fine Georgian Gothic staircase and ceilings were added in the eighteenth century. Family portraits and interesting furniture, including a fine collection of Georgian chairs in the Gothic taste. The park contains exceptional avenues of Spanish chestnut (400 years old), oak and beech and an Iron Age fort from which fourteen counties can be seen on a clear day.

Open: April and October: Saturday, and Sundays 2 – 5 p.m.; Easter Saturday, Sunday and Monday, 2 – 6 p.m.; May to end September, Wednesday to Sunday and Bank Holiday Monday, 2 – 6 p.m. Last admissions half hour before closing.

Admission: Adult: £2.70; Family Ticket: £7.40.

Facilities: Free car parking.

Disabled Access: Access to ground floor only and part of grounds; special parking by castle.

Additional Information: Dogs in parkland on leads only, picnics welcome in parkland only.

DARTMOUTH CASTLE

Dartmouth Castle, Castle Road, Dartmouth, Devon, TQ6 0JN.
(0803) 833588

Status: English Heritage.

General Description: Jutting out into the narrow entrance to the Dart estuary, with the sea lapping at its foot and steep, wooded slopes climbing up from behind, Dartmouth Castle was well positioned to guard what was once one of England's important trading ports. It was the first English castle to be constructed with artillery in mind, and has a number of cannons positioned to give an impression of preparation for war. Many fortifications have been added and altered over the past 450 years. An example can be seen in the restored coastal defence battery fully equipped with guns.

Open: Good Friday or 1st April (whichever is earlier) to 30th September; open daily, 10 a.m. – 6 p.m. 1st October to Maundy Thursday or 31st March (whichever is earlier), open Tuesday to Sunday, 10 a.m. – 4 p.m.

Admission: Adults: £1.30; Senior Citizens/Students/UB40 Holders: 95p; Children: 65p; English Heritage Members free. Special party rates.

Facilities: Car park, coach park in Dartmouth, gift shop, toilets.

DEAL CASTLE

Victoria Road, Deal, Kent.
(0304) 372762

Ownership: Crown Property in care of English Heritage.

Status: English Heritage.

General Description: The largest of Henry VIII's forts, Deal Castle still has a captain resident at times. The castle is built in the shape of the Tudor Rose. Anne of Cleves had her first meal here before going to see Henry.

Open: 1st October to Maundy Thursday, 10 a.m. – 4 p.m. Closed lunch 1 – 2 p.m. Good Friday to 30th September, 10 a.m. – 6 p.m.

Admission: Adults: £1.80; Concessions: £1.20; Children: 80p.

Facilities: Free audio tour.

Disabled Access: Limited access.

Additional Information: No dogs, picnic areas, soft drinks/ices/biscuits available in gift shop.

DOVER CASTLE

Dover, Kent, CT16 1HU.
(0304) 201628

Ownership: English Heritage.

Status: English Heritage.

General Description: As you wander around the castle, you
will discover many reminders of a glorious past, from Iron
Age to World War II. Climb the spiral stairs to the roof of the
keep and survey the surrounding scene as lookouts have done
over the centuries. Explore the underground passages,
originally dug in 1216 at the time of an attack by Prince
Louis of France and extended during the Napoleonic Wars.
Passages in another part of the castle played an important
tactical role in World War II. The natural defensive
properties of the site were recognised in pre-historic times.
The Romans also saw its importance. A solitary relic of their
times at Dover can be seen next to the Saxon church of St.
Mary of Castro. It is a rare Pharos or Roman lighthouse – the
only example in Europe. The Normans fortified at Dover,
though little remains, Henry II began the building of the great
keep and the castle was substantially completed in the reign
of Henry III. In the eighteenth century alterations to the
towers improved the line of the fire and in the nineteenth
century the underground fortifications were improved. The
castle's involvements in World War II completed the
remarkable saga of its contribution to the defence of England.

Open: Summer: Good Friday or 1st April (whichever is
earlier) to 30th September, daily, 10 a.m. to 6 p.m. Winter:
1st October to Maundy Thursday or 31st March (whichever is

earlier), daily, 10 a.m. – 5 p.m. Closed 24th to 26th December and 1st January.

Admission: Adults: £4.50; Senior Citizens/Students/UB40 holders: £3.40; Children: £2.30.

Facilities: Parking, shop, restaurants.

Disabled Access: Limited disabled facilities, wheelchairs, disabled toilets (hilly site).

Additional Information: Grounds available for picnics, dogs allowed into grounds on leash, but not to inside of buildings.

DUNSTANBURGH CASTLE

Craster, Alnwick, Northumberland.
(0665) 576231

Ownership: Owned by National Trust.

Status: National Trust and English Heritage.

General Description: Dunstanburgh Castle is set majestically on a coastal headland, in a region historically remote and difficult of access. Beneath its walls, stormy seas pound the rocky shoreline; the screams of seabirds echo eerily around its cliffs. A Lancastrian stronghold, the castle was built by the second Earl of Lancaster (Earl Thomas) in 1313-16. It played a significant role during the Wars of the Roses. Twice besieged, it eventually fell to Yorkist troops, in one of the victories of Edward IV that helped establish the House of York on the English throne.

Open: All year, open daily. Summer: Good Friday or 1st April (whichever is earlier) to 30th September, 10 a.m. to 6 p.m. Winter: 1st October to Maundy Thursday or 31st March, 10 a.m. to 6 p.m. closed Mondays, Christmas Eve, Christmas Day, Boxing Day and New Years Day.

Admission: Adults: 95p; Senior Citizens/Students: 75p; Children aged 5 to 16 years: 45p; under 5s free.

Facilities: Parking in Craster 1^1/$_2$ miles, cold drinks and biscuits.

Disabled Access: Limited access.

Additional Information: Large grassed areas for picnics, dogs allowed on lead.

DUNSTER CASTLE

Dunster Near Minehead, Somerset.
(0643) 821314

Ownership: National Trust.

Status: National Trust.

General Description: The fortified house has been the home of the Tuttrell family for 600 years, with the thirteenth-century castle building sited below a Norman motte. In Anglo-Saxon times it served as a frontier fortress against the Celts and Northmen. Major additions and alterations to the castle were carried out during the sixteenth, eighteenth and nineteenth centuries, the latter-century being the period in which the famous architect Anthony Salwin gave the house its castellated appearance. During the Civil War it was besieged and slighted by Oliver Cromwell. Prominent features of the house include a magnificent dining room ceiling. Also of note is the elaborately carved oak staircase and the leather gallery with its unique wall hangings. The Tuttrells consolidated their ancestral home at East Quantoxhead in 1974 and the castle was given by them to the National Trust in 1976.

Open: Castle, garden and park, 1st April to 4th October, daily except Thursday and Friday, 11 a.m. – 5 p.m. October to 1st November, daily except Thursday and Friday, 11 a.m. – 4 p.m.

Admission: Adults: £4.30; Children: £2.10. Party: £3.80.

Facilities: Parking facilities, special parking by
arrangement, National Trust shop and tea-rooms by water
mill.

Disabled Access: Batri-car available and welcoming
assistance by stewards. Special parking by arrangement.

Additional Information: Picnic area adjacent to car park.
Dogs prohibited from gardens, but if on lead allowed in park
area.

DURHAM CASTLE

The Castle, Durham, DH1 3RL.
(091) 374 3864

Ownership: University of Durham.

General Description: Norman foundation (1070s) and the home of the Prince Bishop of Durham until 1832, the Castle is a Grade 1 Listed Building and, with the Cathedral, a World Heritage site. Standing on a peninsular of the River Wear above Durham City, it is a fine example of a Motte and Baillie Castle with a Great Hall (1284) Tudor kitchens (1499), Norman Chapel (1070s), Tunstall Chapel (1540s), Courtyard, Keep and Barbican. Guided tours are given daily.

Open: July to September, daily, 10 a.m. – 4.30 p.m. Other times: Monday, Wednesday, Friday 2 p.m. – 4.30 p.m.

Admission: Guided tour: £1.20; Group rate: £1, Children: half price.

Facilities: Parking nearby, food and accommodation in vocatious, conferences and banqueting.

Disabled Access: Limited access.

EASTNOR CASTLE

Eastnor Castle, Near Ledbury, Herefordshire, HR8 1RN.
(0531) 2302/2849 Administrator – (0684) 567103 or (0531) 3160

Ownership: Eastnor Castle Estates Company.

Status: Historic Houses Association.

General Description: With its massed towers, castellated terraces, lake, magnificent forty acre arboretum and 500 acre deer park set within the dramatic landscape of the Malvern Hills, Eastnor Castle captures the spirit of medieval chivalry and romance. The castle is the home of the Hervey-Bathurst's and their young children, descendants of the first Earl Somers who built the castle in 1812. The sumptuous interiors display a superb collection of armour, fine tapestries, Italian and Gothic furniture, together with old master paintings by Kneller, Van Dyck, Romney, Watts and many others. Eastnor Castle has been the location for a number of popular T.V. films and programmes.

Open: Bank Holiday Sundays and Mondays. Sundays beginning May to middle October. Tuesdays, Wednesdays and Thursdays in July and August, 2 p.m. to 5 p.m.

Admission: Adults: £3.00; Children: £1.25 castle and grounds. Adults: £1.50; Children: 75p grounds only.

Facilities: Parking for 70 to 80 cars, tearoom for light lunches and cream teas, coaches welcome.

Disabled Access: None at present.

Additional Information: Picnics in grounds and car park, dogs allowed in castle on leads.

FARLEIGH HUNGERFORD CASTLE

*Farleigh Hungerford Castle, Farleigh Hungerford, Near Bath,
Somerset, BA3 6RS
(0225) 754026*

Ownership: English Heritage.

General Description: Extensive ruins remain of this
fourteenth-century castle. Best preserved is the former chapel
which boasts memorials with effigies of the Hungerford
family, fine stained glass windows, wall paintings. The crypt
contains eight lead coffins (mummified). The museum houses
many excavated archaeological finds and armour mostly from
the Civil War period. Special events held most weekends
during the summer.

Open: Good Friday or 1st April (whichever is earlier) to 30th
September, open daily, 10 a.m. – 6 p.m. 1st October to
Maundy Thursday or 31st March, open Tuesday to Sunday,
10 a.m. – 4 p.m.

Admission: Adult: 95p; Senior Citizens: 75p; Children over
5: 45p; Education visits to school on booking in advance;
Coach parties welcome.

Facilities: Car park, coach parking.

Disabled Access: Outside areas only.

Additional Information: Picnics are allowed, dogs must be
kept on leads.

FARNHAM CASTLE

Farnham, Surrey, GU9 0AG.
(0252) 721194

Ownership: Church Commissioners.

General Description: The castle was founded in 1138 A.D. by Henry de Blois, the grandson of William the Conqueror. It was the home of the Bishops of Winchester and of Guildford for over 800 years. During those centuries it was greatly extended and at times reconstructed so that its architecture reflects the changing styles of successive periods of history. Farnham Castle is the home of the Centre for International Briefing, a unique organisation providing residential courses for people from all walks of life, who are about to go overseas to work or live. It is now adapted to the needs of the Centre providing pleasant accommodation for seventy-two people.

Open: Wednesdays 2 p.m. – 4 p.m. (not Christmas week).

Admission: Adults: £1, Child/Student/Senior Citizens: 50p; Groups of adults: 75p; Groups of children/Students/Senior Citizens: 40p.

Facilities: Parking.

Disabled Access: Limited access.

FRAMLINGHAM CASTLE

Framlingham, Woodbridge, Suffolk, IP13 9BP.
(0728) 724189

Ownership: Pembroke College, Cambridge.

Status: English Heritage.

General Description: A superb twelfth-century castle, which from the outside looks almost the same as when it was built. From the continuous curtain wall, linking thirteen towers, there are excellent views over Framlingham, and the charming reed-fringed mere. At different times, the castle has been a fortress, an Elizabethan prison, a poor house, and a school. The many alterations over the years have led to a pleasing mixture of historical styles.

Open: Good Friday or 1st April (whichever is earlier) to 30th September, open daily, 10 a.m. – 6 p.m. 1st October to Maundy Thursday or 31st March (whichever is earlier), open Tuesday to Sunday, 10 a.m. – 4 p.m.

Admission: Adults: £1.30; Senior Citizens/Students/UB40: 94p; Children: 65p; Under 5's: free.

Facilities: Parking 50 yards from castle entrance. Tea room nearby but not at property. Education room for schools.

Disabled Access: Disabled access to ground floor only. Disabled toilet in town, 200 yards away.

Additional Information: Dogs are allowed inside the castle, and lots of walks around outside grounds. Plenty of picnic space too in grounds.

GUILDFORD CASTLE KEEP

Castle Grounds, Castle Street, Guildford, Surrey, GU1 3TU.
(0483) 444701

Ownership: Guildford Borough Council.

Status: English Heritage.

General Description: The most impressive of the ruins of
Guildford Castle is the great square Norman keep, standing
on its mound it dominates the centre of the picturesque old
town. It was the only royal castle in Surrey, however, it is not
one of those that have left a mark in British history. Its
heyday lasted barely a century and it was largely neglected
during the great castle building period under Edward I and
later. It was virtually a ruin by the end of the Middle Ages.
However, this lack of later building means that it is a rare
example of a Norman and early Plantagenet castle
uncomplicated by subsequent work. Built mainly of local
Bargate stone the castle was a popular residence for royalty
in the thirteenth century, King John and Henry III being
frequent visitors.

Open: April to September, daily, 10.30 a.m. – 6.00 p.m.

Admission: Adults: 65p; Children: 35p.

Disabled Access: Grounds only.

Additional Information: Lawns in grounds may be used for
picnics, dogs allowed but must be kept on leash.

HASTINGS CASTLE

Castle Hill Road, West Hill, Hastings, East Sussex.
(0424) 718888

General Description: It was the Normans invading Britain in 1066 who took advantage of the commanding hill which overlooked the port of Hastings, erecting the first of their prefabricated wooden fortresses, to be replaced by stone following the Conquest. An exciting twenty minute audio-visual programme 'The 1066 Story', in the Castle Grounds, covers 1066 and the Norman Conquest as well as the history of Hasting Castle through the centuries. The theatre, designed as a medieval siege tent, seats up to seventy people. The majestic ruins of Hastings Castle command panoramic views of the town, and include such interesting features as the Whispering Dungeons, and the once magnificent Eastern Gateway where you can still see the slots for the portcullis. An unusual approach to the Castle can be made by the West Cliffe Railway, which climbs from street level, inside the hill, to emerge near the Castle entrance.

Open: April 11th to September 27th, daily, 10 a.m. – 5 p.m. September 28th to November 1st, daily, 11 a.m. – 4 p.m. For winter opening times telephone (0424) 422964.

Admission: Adult: £2; Senior Citizens: £1.75; Child: £1.50; Family: £6.50.

Facilities: Street parking nearby, souvenir shop, guide book available.

Disabled Access: Not suitable for wheelchairs.

HEDINGHAM CASTLE

Castle Hedingham, Near Halstead, Essex, CO9 3DJ.
(0787) 60261

Ownership: The Hon. Thomas Lindsay.

Status: Private ownership.

General Description: One of the finest and best preserved Norman keeps in England, built by Aubrey de Vere in 1140 and home of the de Veres, Earls of Oxford, Lord Great Chamberlains of England, for 550 years. Besieged by King John and visited by King Henry VII, King Henry VIII and Queen Elizabeth I, the Castle is of great historical interest and is still owned by a descendant of the Earls of Oxford. In the banqueting hall there is fine decorative stone work, and the magnificent arch supporting the ceiling is a tribute to the skill of the Norman masons. The beauty of this splendid room can also be enjoyed from the Minstrels' Gallery, built within the thickness of the ten foot walls. The Castle is approached by a beautiful Tudor Bridge, which spans the dry moat surrounding the inner bailey. This was built in 1496 to replace the drawbridge by the Thirteenth Earl of Oxford, one of Henry VII's chief Commanders at the Battle of Bosworth. The Garrison Chamber was home to the soldiers, armourers and bowmen, this Guard room is now hung with the banners of those who played an important part in the long history of the Castle. Home made cakes and light refreshments are now available here. There are lovely walks around the lake and in the peaceful woodland surrounding the Castle. Hedingham Castle is situated one mile off the A604 between Cambridge and Colchester.

Open: Easter to end of October daily 10 a.m. – 5 p.m.

Admission: Adults: £2.25; Children: £1.50.

Facilities: Good parking, light refreshments.

Disabled Access: Limited.

Additional Information: Picnic tables, dogs on leads.

HELMSLEY CASTLE

Helmsley, North Yorkshire, YO6 5AB.
(0439) 70442

Status: English Heritage.

General Description: Close to the market square, with a view of the town, is this twelfth-century castle. Spectacular earthworks surround a great ruined keep dating from the Norman Conquest. There is an exhibition and tableau on the history of the castle.

Open: April to September, daily, 10 a.m. – 6 p.m.
October to March, Tuesday to Sunday, 10 a.m. – 4 p.m.

Admission: Adult: £1.50; Concession: £1.10; Child: 75p.

Facilities: Car park nearby.

Additional Information: Dogs allowed in some areas.

HEMYOCK CASTLE

Hemyock Castle, Hemyock, Cullompton, Devon, EX15 3RJ.
(0823) 680745

Ownership: Captain W. W., Mrs. P. M., and Dr. Margaret Sheppard.

Status: Private Ownership.

General Description: Set in the Blackdown Hills in the River Culm Valley (recently declared an Area of Outstanding Natural Beauty) Hemyock meant 'summer springs' to our Celtic ancestors, who could always be sure of water for their livestock. Soon after the Norman Conquest the Hidon family dwelt in a fortified moated manor house – later inherited by the powerful Dynham family. In 1380 Richard II gave permission to crenellate the castle with towers forty feet high. 300 years later the castle passed to the influential Parliamentarian Popham family. The castle changed hands several times until after the Restoration, when Charles II ordered it to be 'slighted' in common with several other castles. Farm and ruins were purchased by General John Graves Simcoe (first Lieutenant Governor, Upper Canada, Founder of Toronto) in the late eighteenth century. He intended to restore Hemyock to its former Medieval glory, but was forestalled by threat of Napoleon's invasion, and later his own untimely death. You may now see the remains of eight towers and the moat. Displays in old farm buildings of pottery shards dug up on site. Early twentieth-century farm yard memorabilia, including Land Army girl at work. Interpretation Centre with life-sized tableaux illustrating main historical events.

Open: From Easter to end of September, Sundays and Bank Holidays, 2 p.m. – 5 p.m., also in July and August, Tuesday and Thursdays, 2 p.m. – 5 p.m. Schools and groups welcome all seasons (by arrangement).

Admission: Adults: £1; Children: 50p; Special group rates.

Facilities: Toilets, picnic area near Catharine Wheel public house. Small car park (one coach), light refreshments, bookable for parties.

Disabled Access: Disabled access to all parts except tower steps, disabled toilet 200 yards (in village).

Additional Information: Picnic area, no dogs allowed as there are free range poultry, ducks, geese etc.

HERTFORD CASTLE

Castle Street, Hertford, Herts, SG14 1HR.
(0992) 552885

Ownership: Owned by Lord Salisbury, leased to East
Hertfordshire District Council.

General Description: After the Conquest, the Normans
constructed a motte and bailey castle near the ford over the
River Lee at Hertford. The large motte still exists today as
does the stone curtain wall constructed in the reign of Henry
II. In 1216 a French Army besieged and captured the Castle.
From Saxon times to the reign of Elizabeth I most monarchs
visited Hertford; coins were minted, charters issued. The
Kings of France and of Scotland were held prisoner in the
Castle in the 1350s. Around 1464 Edward IV rebuilt the
gatehouse ('The Castle' today) and early brickwork is still
visible. The wooden Royal apartments within the
fortifications disappeared long ago. The Stuart Kings granted
the Castle to the second Earl Salisbury and it was used as a
school, as a private residence and, since 1911, as offices of
the local councils, though still the property of Lord Salisbury.

Open: First Sunday in the month from May to September
inclusive, 2.30 p.m. – 4.30 p.m. Band Concert in grounds
3 p.m. – 5 p.m.

Admission: Free.

Facilities: Parking nearby.

Disabled Access: Disabled access ground floor only, disabled
toilets nearby.

HEVER CASTLE

Near Edenbridge, Kent, TN8 7NG.
(0732) 865224

Ownership: Broadland Properties Ltd.

Status: Historic Houses Association.

General Description: Enchanting thirteenth-century double-moated castle, childhood home of Anne Boleyn. Set in magnificent gardens of thirty acres. The gardens feature fine topiary including a maze. The unique Italian Garden with statuary and sculpture dating back 2,000 years and a thirty-five acre lake alongside which visitors can walk and picnic. The castle was restored and filled with treasures by William Waldorf Astor in 1903.

Open: Open daily from 17th March to 8th November. The gardens at 11 a.m. and the castle at 12 noon. Last entry at 5 p.m., final exit 6 p.m. Open for pre-booked private guided tours during the winter.

Admission: Individual rates. Castle and Gardens – Adult: £4.80; Senior Citizen: £4.30; Child (5-16): £2.40; Family ticket: £12.00. Gardens only – Adult: £3.40; Senior Citizen: £2.90; Child (5-16): £2.00; Family ticket: £8.80. (Group rates available minimum 15 people).

Facilities: Free parking for coaches and cars. Licensed self-service restaurant. Book, gift and garden shop.

Disabled Access: Most of the gardens are accessible for wheelchair visitors. Steps are ramped as is access into the restaurant. No ramps into castle and only ground floor suitable for disabled visitors. Disabled toilets and a few wheelchairs available.

Additional Information: Dogs welcome on leads in gardens only. Picnics permitted in grounds. Bands play on summer Sunday afternoons. June to September open air theatre season. Regular special events – ring for details.

Hurst Castle

Keyhaven, Solent, Hampshire.
(0590) 642544

Ownership: English Heritage.

Status: English Heritage.

General Description: At one time the deadly firepower of
the Solent's western sentinel made it the pride of England's
coastal defences. The fortress of Hurst Castle was one of the
most sophisticated built by Henry VIII. It was intended to
defend England against the French and Spanish should they
invade. No attack came then, but the threat was still real
enough in Victorian times to warrant transforming the castle
into a glowering fortress commanding the narrow entrance to
the Solent. Even now, the ebb and flow of the tides creates
such strong currents that vessels are often halted opposite
Hurst Castle while attempting passage. At time of war such
ships would have been at the mercy of the fort's immense and
formidable firepower. Exhibition about the castle and its
history; you can see two of the recently salvaged huge 38-ton
guns which armed the Victorian fort.

Open: 1st April to 30th September, daily, 10 a.m. – 6 p.m.
1st October to 31st March, weekends only, 10 a.m. – 4 p.m.

Admission: Adults: £1.50; Senior Citizens: £1.10; Students:
£1.10; UB40 holders: £1.10; Children: 75p.

Facilities: Castle reached by two mile walk along shingle split or by boat from Keyhaven, parking at end of split. Restaurant during summer season, toilets.

Additional Information: Dogs allowed, picnics outside castle walls.

KENILWORTH CASTLE

Kenilworth, Warwickshire, CV8 1NE.
(0926) 52078

Ownership: English Heritage.

General Description: Eleventh-century keep built by Henry I's Chamberlain on site of motte and bailey. Added to by some of the most powerful royals and earls including John of Gaunt's Great Hall, Robert Dudley's Elizabethan apartment, Gatehouse and Barn. Curtain walls and towers completed in time of King John. Occupied and altered by Henry V and Henry VIII. The castle is now in ruins, spoilt after Civil War by Commonwealth Parliament.

Open: Open Good Friday to 30th September, 10 a.m. – 6 p.m. 1st October to Easter, 10 a.m. to 4 p.m. Closed Mondays, closed Christmas Eve, Christmas Day, Boxing Day, New Years Day.

Admission: Adults: £1.30; Senior Citizens: 95p; Juniors (under 16): 65p.

Facilities: Car park at south of castle, coach park, toilets; shop, audio tape hire, exhibition in barn.

Disabled Access: Disabled access to ground level of site.

Additional Information: Dogs on leads, picnics allowed.

KIRBY MUXLOE CASTLE

Oakcroft Avenue, Kirby Muxloe, Leicester.
(0533) 386886

Ownership: English Heritage.

Status: English Heritage.

General Description: Built in 1481 by Lord William Hasting. He was beheaded in 1483 by Richard III, no other building was carried out after his death. It was one of the first brick buildings of its kind, and there is a fine example of brickwork in the spiral staircases, especially the staircase in the west tower and in the pattern of blue brick on the outside walls, which show part of the crest of Lord William Hastings.

Open: All year daily. Summer times, 10 a.m. – 6 p.m. Winter times, daily except Mondays, 10 a.m. – 4 p.m.

Admission: At this time, subject to change. Adults: 95p; Reduced: 75p; Children over 5 years: 45p.

Facilities: Restaurants nearby.

Disabled Access: On ground level.

KNARESBOROUGH CASTLE

Castle Yard, Knaresborough, North Yorks.
(0423) 503310

Ownership: Leased by Harrogate Borough Council. Owned by The Duchy of Lancaster.

Status: Run by Local Authority.

General Description: The little known remains of Knaresborough Castle are set high upon a cliff overlooking the River Nidd. The surviving medieval buildings were the fourteenth-century keep, built for Edward II; a subterranean sallyport (or underground tunnel) used for secret excursions; and the old Courthouse which serves as the town's museum, and still houses its original early seventeenth-century Courtroom furniture. The Castle was built as a centre for the administration of the Royal Forest of Knaresborough, but was never far from Royal affairs. The murderers of Thomas à Becket took refuge here, King John spent large sums on building, and Richard II was held as prisoner. The Castle was at the apex of its Royal Favour in the mid-fourteenth century when Queen Philippa spent many summers here. The Castle was besieged after the battle of Marston Moor in 1644, and was dismantled on the order of Parliament in 1648.

Open: Easter weekend, early Spring Bank Holiday to September 30th. Daily 10.30 a.m. to 5 p.m.

Admission: Adults: 70p; Children: 35p; Local residents free.

Facilities: Parking (free) in castle yard, cafes nearby.

Disabled Access: Full disabled access to museum by prior arrangement, access to keep ground floor only for wheelchair users.

Additional Information: Picnics and dogs allowed within castle grounds, no dogs in castle buildings.

LANCASTER CASTLE

Castle Parade, Lancaster, LA1 1YJ.
(0524) 64998

Ownership: Duchy of Lancaster, leased to Lancaster County Council.

Status: Department of Property Services, Lancaster County Council (Duchy of Lancaster Estates).

General Description: The castle, part of which is still used as a prison, dates back to 1100 when it is thought the Great Keep or Lungess Tower was built. The tour visitors to the castle take includes: the Shire Hall, with its collection of coats of arms of the Monarchs, Constables of the Castle, and High Sheriffs; Hadrians Tower with prison implements around its walls; a Roman altar which dates from 120 A.D. the old cells, the Crown Court, still used as a court room, built in 1800; the Drop Room where prisoners were prepared for execution; finally the Grand Jury Room with gillow furniture from the eighteenth century.

Open: Open Easter to September 30th daily. Partial tours when courts are sitting, full tours every weekend and during the month of August.

Admission: Full Tour – Adults: £1.00; Child: 50p.
Partial Tour – Adults: 80p; Child: 40p.

Facilities: City car parks close by, parking at the castle during August.

Disabled Access: Very limited. It is advisable to ring before visiting in order to arrange free parking in precincts.

Additional Information: No dogs allowed in the building (except guide dogs), picnic areas outside.

LAUNCESTON CASTLE

Launceston, Cornwall, PL15 7DR.
(0566) 772365

Ownership: Duchy of Cornwall.

Status: English Heritage.

General Description: Launceston Castle was built in the early years of the Norman Conquest. It commanded the country between Dartmoor and Bodmin Moor, and overlooked the main crossing point of the River Tamar, Cornwall's natural county boundary. The original castle was of timber and earthwork construction, and Motte and Bailey in design. Construction in stone came later in the twelfth century, but more so in the thirteenth when it was re-modelled by Richard Earl of Cornwall. The castle's present high motte and rectangular bailey preserve the original shape of the earlier Norman structure. Of special interest are the unusual stone structures on the motte, a shell keep with a high round tower built within. From Norman times the castle was the principle seat and centre of administration for the Earls (later Dukes) of Cornwall.

Open: All year. Summer: Good Friday or 1st April (whichever is earlier) to 30th September, daily, 10 a.m. – 6 p.m. Winter: 1st October to Maundy Thursday or 31st March, 6 days Tuesday to Sunday, 10 a.m. – 4 p.m.

Admission: Adult: £1.10; Concession: 85p; Child: 55p.

Facilities: Parking close by in the town, small gift shop, site exhibition.

Disabled Access: Disabled access – outer bailey only.

Additional Information: Dogs allowed on lead, picnics welcome (no tables).

LEEDS CASTLE

Maidstone, Kent, ME17 1PL.
(0622) 765400

Ownership: The Castle was bequeathed by the late Hon.
Lady Baillie to the Leeds Castle Foundation in 1974.

Status: The Leeds Castle Foundation.

General Description: Surrounded by 500 acres of
magnificent parkland and gardens, and built on two small
islands in the middle of a natural lake, Leeds Castle is one of
England's oldest and most romantic stately homes. Originally
a Saxon fortress built in A.D. 857, it was rebuilt by the
Normans and later converted to a Royal Palace by King
Henry VIII. For some 300 years, the Castle was a favourite
country palace of the Kings, and especially the Queens, of
medieval England. Often referred to as the Lady's Castle, six
of England's medieval Queens resided here. Now lovingly
restored and beautifully furnished, the Castle contains a
magnificent collection of medieval furnishings, French and
English furniture, tapestries and paintings. Visitors also
delight in seeing the beautiful gardens, including the Russell
Page designed Culpeper Garden and a young maze and
underground grotto.

Open: 16th March to 31st October 1992, everyday, 11 a.m. –
5 p.m.*. November to mid-March, weekends, 11 a.m. –
4 p.m.*. Also daily in Christmas week – 26th December – 1st
January. Latest admission to grounds.

Admission: Castle and Park – Adults: £6.20; Senior
Citizens/Students: £5.20; Children (5 – 15 years inclusive):
£4.20; Family Ticket (2 adults and 2 children): £17. Park and
Gardens – Adults: £4.70; Senior Citizens/Students: £3.70;
Children (5 – 15 years inclusive): £2.70; Family Ticket (2
adults and 2 children): £12.50.

Facilities: Free car parking. Hot and cold meals available on
Castle open days from seventeenth-century oak-beamed tithe
barn, The Fairfax Hall. Guides are present in each room in
the Castle. Private visits can be arranged for groups outside
normal opening hours. Additional attractions to the Castle
include: Duckery, Woodland Garden, Barbican and Fortified
Mill, Dog Collar Museum, Culpeper Garden, greenhouses
and vineyard, maze and secret grotto. Nine hole golf course.

Disabled Access: Special facilities include: wheelchair lift
inside the Castle enabling a full tour of the ground floor;
induction loops in two rooms; an information sheet in braille
in the Dog Collar Museum; wheelchairs (max 6) for loan;
special transport from main parking areas to point near the
Castle; ramps where necessary in grounds; purpose–built
toilets in grounds. Special disabled rate – in addition, helpers
are admitted free on ratio of 1:1.

Additional Information: Picnic sites are located in the park
near the main entrance. Unfortunately, dogs are not allowed
due to free roaming wildfowl. A full range of Special Events
takes place at the Castle during the course of the year –
including enormously popular Open Air Concerts, a Balloon
and Bentley Fiesta, Festival of English Wines and Flower
Festivals.

LEWES CASTLE

Barbican House, 169 High Street, Lewes, East Sussex, BN7 1YE.
(0273) 474379

Ownership: Sussex Archeological Society.

General Description: Lewes Castle was built soon after the
Norman Conquest by William de Warenne a trusted follower
of William the Conqueror. It is one of the earliest stone-built
castles c.1100. The Norman shell keep on the main motte
survives together with sections of the defensive curtain walls
and dry moat, and also a second motte, a very unusual
feature. Two polygonal towers were added to the keep at
about the time of the Battle of Lewes, 1264, when a Barons'
army led by Simon de Montfort defeated Henry III. The
barbican gateway was built by the last of the de Warenne
Earls of Sussex in the fourteenth century. At his death the
main castle buildings fell quickly into disrepair. From the
Castle visitors can enjoy magnificent views across Lewes and
the surrounding countryside.

Open: January to December, Monday to Saturday, 10 a.m. –
5.30 p.m. (last tickets at 5 p.m.). Sunday and Bank Holidays,
11 a.m. – 5.30 p.m.

Admission: Combined admission with Lewes Living History
Model and Museum of Sussex Archaeology – Adult: £2.80;
Child: £1.40; Group and family concessions.

Facilities: Audio-visual show, light refreshments.

Disabled Access: Difficult except to audio-visual.

Additional Information: Picnics in grounds, dogs on leads in
grounds.

LINCOLN CASTLE

Castle Hill, Lincoln, LN1 3AA.
(0522) 511068

Ownership: Lincolnshire County Council.

General Description: Situated close to Lincoln's spectacular medieval cathedral, Lincoln Castle is a Norman motte and bailey Castle built 1068. The wall walks are accessible and offer spectacular views of the historic town and surrounding countryside. Encompassed within the walls is a preserved victorian prison. The unique prison chapel (open to the public) consists of rows of cubicles where the prisoners were separately enclosed, unable to see anyone except the minister.

Open: All year except Christmas Day, Boxing Day, New Year's Day, Monday to Saturday, 9.30 a.m. – 5.30 p.m. Sunday, 11.00 a.m. – 5.30 p.m. Winter closing 4.00 p.m.

Admission: Adults: £1.00; Child/Senior Citizens/Student: 80p; Party rates on application. These prices are not applicable on event days.

Facilities: Video – *The Lincoln Castle Story.*

Disabled Access: Disabled ramps, nearest disable toilet Castle Hill.

Additional Information: No dogs, picnic areas.

LUDLOW CASTLE

Ludlow, Shropshire.
(0584) 873947

Ownership: The Trustees of the Powis Castle Estate.

General Description: Ludlow Castle dates from about 1086 and was owned by Marcher Lords until, in 1472, Edward IV sent the infant Prince of Wales and his brother (the Princes in the Tower) to live there. At the same time the Council for Wales and the Marches was established in Ludlow so the Castle became both a royal palace and a seat of government. Prince Arthur, eldest son of Henry Tudor, also lived at the Castle for a time with his bride, Catherine of Aragon. In 1689 the Royal Welch Fusiliers were founded at Ludlow by Lord Herbert of Chirbury but after the Civil War the Castle was deserted and in 1811 was bought from the Crown as a ruin by the 1st Earl of Powis. A bridge from the huge outer bailey leads to the inner bailey containing the remains of Norman, medieval and Tudor buildings including the Chapel, with its Norman arches. Milton's 'Comus' was first performed in the Castle in 1634 and a Shakespearean play is now performed there each June as part of the Ludlow Festival.

Open: Daily 1st February to 30th April, 10.30 a.m. – 4 p.m. 1st May to 30th September, 10.30 a.m. to 5 p.m. 1st October to 30th November, 10.30 a.m. to 4 p.m. Closed December and January.

Admission: Adults: £2.00; Children: £1.00; Senior Citizens: £1.50; Family: £6.00.

Facilities: Parking and cafes in adjacent Castle Square.
Disabled Access: Access for disabled visitors at ground level.
Additional Information: Picnics and dogs allowed.

LULLINGSTONE CASTLE

Eynsford, Kent.
(0322) 862114

Ownership: Guy Hart Dyke.

General Description: The buildings comprising the castle
consist of the brick gatehouse built in the reign of Henry VII,
the mansion house of Queen Anne period in appearance but
most of which is of Tudor origin, and the fourteenth-century
church. Often visited by King Henry VIII and Queen Anne,
friends of the resident squires at the time, Lullingstone Castle
has remained the seat of the Hart Dyke family and their
antecedents since it was built in 1497.

Open: April to the end of October, Saturdays, Sundays and
Bank Holidays, 2 p.m. – 6 p.m. Wednesdays, Thursdays,
Fridays by arrangement.

Admission: Adult: £3; Senior Citizen: £2.50; Child: £1.

Facilities: Free car parking, refreshments available in
gatehouse tearooms.

Disabled Access: Ground floor access to house and church.

Additional Information: Picnics are permitted but not dogs.

LYMPNE CASTLE

Hythe, Kent.
(0303) 267571

Ownership: Harry Margary.

General Description: Set on the brink of an inland cliff, picturesque Lympne Castle has a superbly panelled Great Hall with a splendid crown-post roof flanked by a Norman Tower to the east and a Medieval Tower to the west. Features of architectural interest abound and the turret stairways lead to the tops of the towers which command spectacular views across the Romney Marshes and over the sea to France. The Castle was granted in perpetuity by Archbishop Lanfranc (1070-1089) to the Archdeacons of Canterbury. It passed into private ownership in 1870. Since that time, the Castle has been occupied by five families: from 1962 it has been the home of Mr. and Mrs. Harry Margary. In 1908 it was extensively restored by Sir Robert Lorimer, the Scottish architect. Exhibitions, toys, reproduction medieval brasses and scale model English Cathedrals.

Open: Easter weekend to 30th September, every day 10.30 a.m. – 6 p.m. Closed occasionally on Saturdays.

Admission: Adult: £1.50; Child (5-14): 50p.

Facilities: Car park at Castle Gate.

Additional Information: Picnics in garden, dogs on lead.

MIDDLEHAM CASTLE

Middleham, Leyburn, North Yorkshire, DL8 4QR.
(0969) 23899

Status: English Heritage.

General Description: This childhood home of Richard III stands on the edge of Wensleydale moorland. There is a massive twelfth-century keep standing within later fortifications.

Open: April to September, daily, 10 a.m. – 6 p.m. October to March, Tuesday to Sunday, 10 a.m. – 4 p.m.

Admission: Adult: £1.10; Concession: 85p; Child: 55p; English Heritage members free.

Additional Information: Shop, suitable for picnics, dogs allowed.

NEWARK CASTLE

Castlegate, Newark, Notts.
(0636) 79403 (Millgate Folk Museum)

Ownership: Newark and Sherwood District Council.

General Description: Parts of the original twelfth-century structure still survive, notably the gatehouse, which is one of the finest examples from its period in the country. Visited by Henry II, King John, Henry III, Edward II, Henry VII, James I. King John died here in 1216. Castle withstood three sieges in the Civil War. Charles retreated here in 1645 after the Battle of Naseby. Castle was partially demolished after defeat of Charles I.

Open: Grounds, all year dawn to dusk. Castle, Easter to November, Tuesday, Wednesday, Friday, Saturday, Sunday afternoons. Gilstrap Interpretation Centre from 2nd May 1992.

Admission: Free.

Facilities: Parking, restaurants close by, displays and souvenir shop in south-west Tower, castle interpretation display due to open May 1992, toilets in grounds.

Disabled Access: Grounds, toilets and new interpretation centre have disabled access.

Additional Information: No dogs.

NORHAM CASTLE

Norham (in Parish of Horn Cliffe), Berwick upon Tweed,
Northumbria, TD15 23Y.
(0289) 382329

Ownership: English Heritage.

Status: English Heritage.

General Description: Built in twelfth-century by a Bishop of
Durham this massive castle stands on a site of great natural
strength. It withstood repeated attacks, in the thirteenth and
fourteenth centuries and was thought to be impregnable, but
in 1513 it was stormed by the forces of James IV of Scotland
and partially destroyed. Although later re-built, the castle lost
its importance as a defensive stronghold by the end of the
sixteenth-century. This is the place where a knight called
Marmion, came to do his Lady Fair great honour by riding
out alone against the Scots. Amazingly he did survive and
later gained his lady's hand in marriage.

Open: Summer, daily, 10 a.m. – 6 p.m. Winter, daily except
Mondays and Tuesdays, 10 a.m. – 4 p.m.

Admission: Adults: £1.10; Concession: 85p; Junior: 55p.

Additional Information: Picnic allowed, dogs allowed on a
lead.

NUNNERY CASTLE

Nunnery, Near Frome, Somerset, BA11 4LQ.
(0373) 836 226

Ownership: R. R. C. Walker.

Status: English Heritage.

General Description: In 1373 the King gave the de la Mare family a permit to crenellate their house into Nunnery Castle, possibly a favour for good work fighting in the Crusades. During the Civil War it was on the Royalists side and eventually it was taken by Cromwell, who fired his artillery on the north weak side and breached the wall. Then Cromwell sacked the Castle and slighted it. 100 years later one of the female side of the owners was allowed to rebuild it, and it was lived in for 100 years. In the late nineteenth century a storm blew down most of the north wall. Carolinean silver and two cannon balls fired by Cromwell were found in the moat. Both were put in the church where one still remains.

Open: Every day all times (24 hours).

Admission: Free.

Facilities: Limited parking for 2 hours in market place, one restaurant and one pub in village.

Additional Information: Picnics, dogs under control allowed. There are no toilets in the village.

OKEHAMPTON CASTLE

Okehampton, Devon, EX20 1JB.
(0837) 52844

Status: English Heritage.

General Description: The ruins of the largest castle in Devon
stand on a knoll above the River West Okement, surrounded
by splendid woodland. Originally a base from which to
subdue the local population after the Norman Conquest,
Okehampton Castle was built with the threat of rebellion very
much in mind. Although the castle was dismantled in the
sixteenth century, there is still a lot to see including the
Norman motte and the remains of the keep. The raised motte
was protected by a gatehouse and a barbican, with a long,
narrow, steep and angled passage running between them
which would have trapped any would-be aggressors.
Nowadays the castle is secluded and a lovely place in which
to relax and unwind.

Open: Good Friday or 1st April (whichever is earlier) to 30th
September, daily, 10 a.m. – 6 p.m. 1st October to Maundy
Thursday or 31st March (whichever is earlier), Tuesday to
Sunday, 10 a.m. – 4 p.m.

Admission: Adults: £1.50; Senior Citizens/Student
Cards/UB40 Cards: £1.10; Children (under 16): 75p; Under 5
years: free. Special party rates. Above include free Walkman
Soundalive Tape Tour.

Facilities: Free car park, large woodland walk, picnic area,
toilets and light refreshments available, shop selling guides,
posters and souvenirs.

Disabled Access: Not suitable as there are steps and steep slopes.

Additional Information: Picnic area, dogs on leads.

PENDENNIS CASTLE

Falmouth, Cornwall, TR11 4LP.
(0326) 316594 or (0326) 212044

Status: English Heritage.

General Description: Well preserved example of the coastal forts erected by Henry VIII – surrounded by late sixteenth-century fortifications. During the Civil War it was captured by the Parliamentary Army after a five month siege. Magnificent views from the grounds and from the roofs of the keep. Video display in lower gun room, sight/sound exhibition with life size models in upper gun room. Walkman tours of the property are available for hire.

Open: 1st April to 30th September, daily, 10 a.m. – 6 p.m. Rest of year 10 a.m. – 4 p.m., closed Mondays.

Admission: Adults: £1.80; Concession: £1.40; Children: 90p; 15% reduction for groups of eleven or more people.

Facilities: Car parking, tea room, sight/sound exhibition, Walkman tours can be hired on site.

Disabled Access: Grounds, souvenir shop, tea room, part of keep.

Additional Information: Space within the grounds for picnics, dogs allowed if on a lead.

PENRITH CASTLE

Status: English Heritage.

General Description: This fourteenth-century castle, set in parkland on the edge of Penrith, was built to defend the town against repeated attacks by Scottish raiders.

Open: All year, accessible during park opening hours, 7.30 a.m. – 9 p.m. all week.

Admission: Free admission.

Facilities: Limited parking.

Disabled Access: Disabled access.

Additional Information: Dogs allowed, toilets.

PEVENSEY CASTLE

Pevensey Castle, Pevensey, East Sussex, BN24 5JP.
(0323) 762604

Ownership: English Heritage.

Status: English Heritage.

General Description: First built as a coastal fort to protect the anchorage used by the Roman fleets, William the Conqueror occupied it when he landed at Pevensey in 1066 before the Battle of Hastings. Since then the castle has been defended against many sieges and attacks and its walls have never been breached. It was made ready to face the enemy once again in 1940. World War II gun emplacements and pill boxes are concealed in the medieval castle and amongst the old Roman bastions. Trace the eras of fortification as you wander round the Roman ruins and enter the courtyard and rooms of the castle through the gatehouse. You will be treading in the footsteps of soldiers from all the centuries of Pevensey's past.

Open: 1st April to 30th September, open daily, 10 a.m. – 1 p.m., 2 p.m. – 6 p.m. 1st October to 31 March, open Tuesday to Sunday, 10 a.m. – 1 p.m., 2 p.m. – 4 p.m.

Admission: Adults: £1.50; Senior Citizens/Students and UB40 holders: £1.10; Children: 75p. Increase in charge when special events on.

Facilities: Soundalive Audio Tour available: £1.00. Parking, toilets nearby, plus castle cottage tea room.

Disabled Access: Partial access for disabled visitors. Disabled toilets nearby.

Additional Information: Picnickers welcome, dogs allowed on leads.

PEVERIL CASTLE

Market Place, Castleton, Near Sheffield, S30 2WX.
(0433) 620613

Ownership: Duchy of Lancaster (The Queen).

Status: English Heritage.

General Description: Norman motte and bailey ruined castle. Commencement of building 1086 for William Peveril, reputed illegitimate son of William the Conqueror. Henry II built the keep in 1176. Fell ruinous after 1400. Reason for having a castle here was to oversee the mining of lead used for William's castle building programme. Later used for a hunting lodge for Royalty in the Peak Forest.

Open: Summer: Easter or 1st April (whichever is earliest) to 31st September, 10 a.m. – 6 p.m. Winter: 1st October to Maundy Thursday or 31st March, 10 a.m. – 4 p.m. Closed Mondays.

Admission: Adults: £1.10; Children under 5 to 16: 55p; Reduced i.e. Pensioners, Students and UB40s: 85p. Free to school parties on application.

Facilities: No parking, no toilets, facilities in village within easy reach.

Additional Information: Picnics, dogs on lead. Steep zig-zag path so sensible footwear advisable.

PICKERING CASTLE

Pickering, North Yorkshire, YO18 7AX.
(0751) 74989

Ownership: Duchy of Lancaster.

Status: English Heritage.

General Description: Standing on the edge of the North Yorkshire Moors Pickering Castle is a splendid castle of motte and bailey design, founded by William the Conqueror. For most of its useful life, however, it controlled hunting in the nearby forest and provided accommodation for the King and his retinue. The castle is well preserved and much of the original walls, tower and keep can still be seen. The ruins, surrounded by trees, stand on a hill, to the north of the town, overlooking Pickering Beck.

Open: Good Friday or 1st April (whichever is earliest) to 30th September, open daily, 10 a.m. – 6 p.m. 1st October to Maundy Thursday or 31st March, open Tuesday to Sunday 10 a.m. – 4 p.m.

Admission: Adults: £1.50; Over 60s/Students/UB40 holders: £1.10; Children 5-15: 75p; Under 5s free.

Facilities: Small car park at castle entrance, toilets in car park, on site shop, education room may be booked by school parties, exhibition in chapel opening 1992.

Disabled Access: Access for disabled visitors (except motte), disabled toilet in car park.

Additional Information: Picnics are allowed inside castle, dogs must be kept on leash.

PORCHESTER CASTLE

215 Castle Street, Fareham, Porchester, Hants, PO16 9QW.
(0705) 378291

Status: English Heritage.

General Description: A residence for Kings and a rallying point for troops, the history of this grand castle stretches back for 2,000 years. There are Roman walls, the most complete in Europe, substantial remains of the Royal castle and an exhibition which tells the story of Porchester.

Open: 1st April to 30th September, open daily, 10 a.m. – 6 p.m. 1st October to 31st March, open Tuesday to Sunday, 10 a.m. – 4 p.m. Closed 24th to 26th December and 1st January.

Admission: Adults: £1.50; Senior Citizens/UB40's/Students: £1.10; Children: 75p.

Facilities: Parking, toilets in car park.

Disabled Access: Access to grounds and lower levels.

Additional Information: Dogs only allowed in certain areas, shop.

POWDERHAM CASTLE

Kenton, Exeter, Devon, EX6 8JQ.
(0626) 890243

Ownership: Lord Courtenay.

Status: Historic Houses Association.

General Description: Built between 1390 and 1420 by Sir Philip Courtenay. Surrounded by a deer park the Castle is situated on the west bank of the River Exe estuary. The Castle was damaged during the Civil War but restored and altered during the eighteenth and nineteenth centuries. It is still the home of the Courtenay family, Earls of Devon. The Castle contains some very fine furniture and paintings as well as very dramatic plasterwork in the Staircase Hall. The Music Room is probably the finest room in the house with regency furniture, Italian marble and an eighteenth-century organ by Bryce Seed of Bristol. An elegant terraced rose garden forms the east front of the Castle and is the home for Timothy a tortoise probably 130 years old.

Open: May to September, closed Fridays and Saturdays.

Facilities: Ample free parking for both cars and coaches, tearoom/restaurant.

Disabled Access: Limited.

Additional Information: There is a picnic area, dogs are allowed in the car park area only and kept on leads due to deer park.

PRUDHOE CASTLE

Prudhoe, Northumberland, NE42 6NA.
(0661) 833459

Status: English Heritage.

General Description: The extensive remains of this twelfth-century castle include a gatehouse, curtain wall and keep. There is much to see, including a video about the castles of Northumbria.

Open: April to September, daily, 10 a.m. – 6 p.m. October to March, Tuesday to Sunday, 10 a.m. – 4 p.m.

Admission: Adult: £1.50; Concession: £1.10; Child: 75p.

Facilities: Parking, video display.

Additional Information: Toilets, dogs allowed.

RABY CASTLE

Staindrop, Darlington, Co Durham, DL2 3AH.
(0833) 60202 (24 hour answerphone)

Ownership: The Rt. Hon. The Lord Barnard, TD.

Status: Historic Homes Association.

General Description: Historic Raby Castle, set in a 200 acre deer park, has been the home of Lord Barnard's family since 1626. Although the first recorded owner of Raby was King Canute in 1031, the present castle was mainly built in the fourteenth century by the powerful Nevill family who owned it until the Rising of the North in 1569, when it was seized by the Crown. Most of the interior now dates from the eighteenth and nineteenth centuries, although many medieval features remain, particularly the kitchen, with its fine collection of copper cooking utensils, which was used daily for over 600 years. Raby contains fine pictures, furniture and china, and visitors can also enjoy the large walled gardens extending to about five acres. Horse drawn vehicles belonging to the family are also on view. Refreshments are available in the tea room and games and souvenirs from the shop.

Open: Easter Saturday to following Wednesday; May and June, Wednesdays and Sundays only. July to September, daily except Saturdays. Bank Holidays (May, Spring and August) open Saturday to Wednesday. Park and Gardens only open, 11 a.m. – 5.30 p.m. Castle open, 1 p.m. – 5 p.m.

Admission: Castle, Park and Gardens – Adult: £2.75; Child: £1.30; Senior Citizens: £2.25; Park and Gardens only – Adult: £1.00; Child: 75p; Senior Citizens: 75p.

Facilities: Free parking for visitors, coach parking free, tearooms serving light refreshments.

Disabled Access: Specially adapted lavatory facilities, disabled visitors may park near car park. Ground floor only of Castle accessible for wheelchair users (slight help needed, staff usually available).

Additional Information: Dogs allowed only to Park, must be on a lead, not permitted in Castle or Gardens, unless guide dogs. Photography and video filming not permitted inside Castle, picnic tables provided.

RICHMOND CASTLE

Richmond, North Yorkshire, DL10 4QW.
(0748) 822493

Status: English Heritage.

General Description: A splendid medieval fortress, with a fine twelfth-century keep and eleventh-century remains of the curtain wall and domestic buildings. From the battlements you can see nearby Easby Abbey. There is an exhibition in the castle.

Open: April to September, daily, 10 a.m. – 6 p.m. October to March, Thursday to Sunday, 10 a.m. – 4 p.m.

Admission: Adult: £1.50; Concession: £1.10; Child: 75p; English Heritage members free.

Disabled Access: Disabled access.

Additional Information: Toilets, suitable for picnics, guidebook, exhibition.

ROCHESTER CASTLE

Rochester-on-Medway, Kent, ME1 1SW.
(0634) 402276

Ownership: Rochester-on-Medway City Council.

Status: English Heritage.

General Description: Built in the late eleventh century to guard the point where the Roman road of Watling Street crossed the River Medway. The size and position of this imposing Norman castle founded on the Roman city walls, eventually made it an important Royal stronghold for several hundred years. The magnificent keep is over 100 feet high with walls twelve feet thick, King John besieged the castle for many weeks during his war with the barons and destroyed one corner of the keep by undermining it. Walk along the battlements and you will enjoy fine views over the river and the surrounding city of Rochester.

Open: Winter: 1st October to Maundy Thursday or 31st March (whichever is earlier), Tuesday to Sunday, 10 a.m. – 4 p.m. Summer: Good Friday or 1st April to 30th September, daily, 10 a.m. – 6 p.m.

Admission: Adult: £1.50; Concessions: £1.10; Child: 75p; 15% discount for groups (eleven or more people).

Facilities: Nearby street parking free, restaurants in Rochester High Street within easy walking distance.

Disabled Access: Disabled toilet in grounds.

Additional Information: Ample room for picnics in grounds, dogs allowed in grounds, not allowed in keep.

ROCKINGHAM CASTLE

Market Harborough, Leics., LE16 8TH.
(0536) 770240

Ownership: Cdr. L. M. M. Saunders Watson DL.

Status: Privately owned.

General Description: Rockingham Castle was built by William the Conqueror and regularly used as a Royal Fortress up to the sixteenth century when Henry VIII granted it to Edward Watson whose family have lived there ever since. The castle covers 900 years of English history from the Council of Rockingham in 1095 through the Civil War, when it housed a Parliamentary Garrison, through the ninteenth century, when Charles Dickens was a frequent visitor, to the present day. It stands on a hill in twelve acres of formal and wild gardens including a rose garden on the site of the medieval keep and a 400 yew hedge. There is a gift shop, home made teas, and an exhibition area.

Open: 1st April (or Easter Sunday if earlier) to 30th September, Sundays and Thursdays, Bank Holiday Mondays and Tuesday following, and Tuesdays during August, 1.30 p.m. – 5.30 p.m.

Admission: House & Gardens: Adults: £3.30; Senior Citizens: £2.70; Children: £2. Gardens only (including Salvin's Tower, Shop, Exhibitionand Tearooms): £2. Special Parties: Adults £2.70 (minimum charge £54.); School parties £1.30 per child (minimum charge for School parties £32.50, one adult free for every 15 children).

Facilities: Free parking, tearooms, exhibition area.

Additional Information: Picnic area, dogs in grounds on leads.

St. Mawes Castle

St. Mawes, Near Truro,Cornwall, TR2 3AA.
(0326) 270526

Ownership: The Crown.

Status: English Heritage.

General Description: The most attractive of Henry VIII's coastal defence forts with a collection of arms, armour and cannonry plus an exhibition of old photographs (local). The castle appears to be impregnable, but in 1646 it was captured by Cromwell's troops without a shot being fired – its guns faced the sea. There are pleasant gardens and most attractive views.

Open: Good Friday (or 1st April) to 31st September, 10 a.m. – 6 p.m. 1st October to Maundy Thursday, 10 a.m. – 4 p.m. (not Mondays).

Admission: Adults: 95p; Senior Citizens/Students/UB40s: 75p; Children (5 years – 15 years inclusive): 45p, Children under 5: free.

Facilities: Limited car parking (free).

Disabled Access: Main entrance floor and gardens only, no charge for the blind, or wheelchair users.

Additional Information: Picnics are permitted in the gardens.

ST. MICHAEL'S MOUNT

Marazion, Cornwall, TR17 0HT.
(0736) 710507

Ownership: Lord St. Levan/National Trust.

Status: National Trust.

General Description: Romantic island castle on top of hill, fourteenth-century chapel, seventeenth- and eighteenth-century rooms, magnificent views, National Trust shop and restaurant, audio visual cinema (video), gardens by arrangement.

Open: Winter: 1st November to end March, Monday, Wednesday and Friday – weather and tide permitting – guided tours 11 a.m., 12 p.m., 2 p.m. and 3 p.m. Phone (0736) 710507 for information.
Summer: 1st April to 31st October, Monday to Friday 10.30 a.m. – 5.30 p.m., last admission 4.45 p.m.

Admission: Per person: £2.90.

Facilities: Parking on mainland, audio visual show, cafe, National Trust restaurant, two shops.

Additional Information: When tide is in ferry boats charge.

SCARBOROUGH CASTLE

Castle Road, Scarborough, North Yorkshire, YO1 1HY.
(0723) 372451

Status: English Heritage.

General Description: From the walls of this enormous twelfth-century castle you will have spectacular coastal views. The walls stretch along the cliff edge, there are also the remains of the three storey high keep and a fourth-century Roman signal station.

Open: April to September, daily, 10 a.m. – 6 p.m.
October to March, Tuesday to Sunday, 10 a.m. – 4 p.m.

Admission: Adult: £1.50; Concession: £1.10; Child: 75p.

Facilities: Audio tours available.

Disabled Access: Disabled access – except keep.

Additional Information: Toilets, suitable for picnics, guidebooks, dogs allowed.

SHERBORNE OLD CASTLE

Castleton, Sherborne, Dorset.
(0935) 812730

Status: English Heritage.

General Description: Norman Bishop's Palace built 1107–35 by Bishop Roger de Caen. Built to an unusual design, with the keep incorporated into the main building, and the outer defences following a symmetrical polygon. Also has a fine Norman window, dating from 1592. Elizabeth I gave the castle to Sir Walter Raleigh in 1594, he moved to Sherborne Lodge in 1642. The castle was held for the King and in 1645 a full scale siege was undertaken by General Fairfax, after sixteen days the castle was surrendered and dismantled. Now it stands a romantic ruin in lovely countryside.

Open: Easter or 1st April (whichever is earlier) to 30th September, daily, 10 a.m. – 6 p.m. Daily except Monday from 1st October to Easter, 10 a.m. – 4 p.m., closed 24th to 26th December and 1st January.

Admission: Adult: 95p; Pensioners, Students: 75p; Children (5 – 16 years): 45p.

Facilities: Parking on grass, no hard standing, site toilets.

Disabled Access: Level site laid to grass, no upper floors on monument open to visitors.

Additional Information: Picnics on all parts of site, dogs allowed on car park grass only.

SIZERGH CASTLE

Near Kendal, Cumbria, LA8 8AE.
(05395) 60070

Ownership: National Trust.

Status: National Trust.

General Description: The Strickland family home for more than 750 years, impressive fourteenth-century pele tower, extended in Tudor times, with some of the finest Elizabethan carved overmantels in the country, good English and French furniture and family portraits surrounded by gardens including the Trust's largest limestone rock garden, good autumn colour.

Open: 1st April to 29th October, Sunday to Thursday, 1.30 p.m. – 5.30 p.m. Garden: as Castle from 12.30 p.m. Last admissions 5.00 p.m.

Admission: Adult: £3.10; Child: £1.60. Parties of fifteen or more £2.30 by arrangement with the Administrator (not Bank Holidays).

Facilities: Parking 100 yards from Castle, tea room open 1.30 p.m. same days as Castle.

Disabled Access: Most of garden mainly via paths. Lower Hall and tea room accessible.

Additional Information: Picnic tables in car park.

SKIPTON CASTLE

Skipton, North Yorkshire, BD23 1AQ.
(0756) 792442

Ownership: Independent.

General Description: The original Norman castle was built
by Robert de Romille in about 1090 to command the valley
of the Upper Aire. In 1310 the castle passed to Robert
Clifford and remained with his family until 1676. Clifford
rebuilt it with a magnificent gatehouse, seven round towers
and a fine curtain wall. The castle was attacked by the Scots,
was in the thick of the Wars of the Roses and, having
withstood a three-year siege in the Civil War, was the last
stronghold in the north to hold out for the King. The damage
was repaired by Lady Anne Clifford, so the castle stands
today a rare survival from Cromwellian destruction. One of
the best preserved medieval castles in England. Over 900
years old and still fully roofed. At its centre lies the beautiful
Conduit Court with Lady Anne's famous yew.

Open: Every day (except Christmas Day): 10 a.m. (Sunday
2 p.m.), last admission 6 p.m. (October to February 4 p.m.)

Admission: Adults: £2.40; Children (5-18 years): £1.20;
Under 5's: Free.

Facilities: Large coach/car park off nearby High Street.

Additional Information: Well behaved dogs allowed, guides
available for pre-booked parties.

STOKESAY CASTLE

Craven Arms, Shropshire, SY7 9AH.
(0588) 672544

Ownership: English Heritage.

Status: English Heritage.

General Description: A superb example of a large, and little altered fortified Manor House built in the late thirteenth century, with an early seventeenth-century gatehouse. The Great Hall is well preserved and there is fine panelling in the solar.

Open: 4th March to 31st October, daily except Tuesday, 10 a.m. – 6 p.m. (5 p.m. in March and October). 1st to 30th November, open weekends only, 10 a.m. – 4 p.m.

Admission: Adults: £2.00; Children under 16: £1.00; No concessions; Children under 5 free.

Facilities: Parking.

Disabled Access: Gardens and Great Hall only.

Additional Information: Toilets, no dogs, parties by appointment.

SUDELEY CASTLE

Winchcombe, Cheltenham, Gloucestershire, GL54 5JD.
(0242) 602308

Ownership: Lady Ashcombe.

Status: Private ownership.

General Description: Sudeley has Royal connections going back to the tenth century. The property of Ethelred the Unready it stayed with the Crown to Tudor times. It became the Palace of Queen Katherine Parr. Henry VIII, Anne Boleyn, Lady Jane Grey and Elizabeth I all stayed at Sudeley. It was also Prince Rupert's campaign headquarters during the Civil War and home to Charles I. Sudeley has many art treasures, paintings by Turner, Rubens, Van Dyck, a collection of lace, arms and armour. Eight magnificent gardens, the centrepiece being the Queen's Garden, a Tudor Knot Garden planted with old fashioned roses and flanked by yew hedges which set off the splendid ruins of the Banqueting Hall.

Open: 1st April to 31st October, 12 noon to 5 p.m.

Admission: Adults/Senior Citizens: £4.75; Child: £2.50; Family: £12.00. Ground: Adults/Senior Citizens: £3.10; Child: £1.40; Group discounts.

Facilities: Car parking, restaurant, coffee shop, craft exhibition, children's play area/fort, moat containing ornamental water fowl, shop, plant centre specialising in old fashioned roses.

Disabled Access: None.

Additional Information: Picnics, collection of lace work, some fine topiary, a Knot Garden, Arms and Civil War Armour.

TAMWORTH CASTLE AND MUSEUM

The Holloway, Tamworth, Staffordshire, B79 7LR.
(0827) 63563

Ownership: Tamworth Borough Council.

General Description: On the site of earlier defences built by
Ethelflaeda Tamworth Castle is a Norman shell-keep of the
motte and bailey type. Polygonal in structure and added to
during eight centuries of almost continual occupancy, the
Castle now has 15 period rooms open to the public, depicting
the lifestyles of its former inhabitants. Especially popular
with visitors are the intermural wall walks, Norman
Exhibition with 'speaking' Knight and haunted bedroom. The
Long Gallery contains artefacts and local collections,
including coins from the local Mint and early photographs,
and there is an audio-visual presentation on Tamworth
history. Within the grounds is a magnificent example of
herringbone masonry and an excavated, double, medieval
gatehouse. The grounds, containing a garden for blind and
disabled visitors, descend down floral terraces to the
confluence of the rivers Tame and Anker.

Open: All year except Christmas Day, Boxing Day and one
other day at New Year.

Admission: Adult: £2.15; Child: 70p; Senior Citizen: £1.15;
Various Concessions; Group rates available.

Facilities: Public parking. AV on local history.

Disabled Access: Disabled access ground floor only, garden
for blind and disabled visitors in grounds.

Additional Information: Dogs not permitted in castle or immediate grounds, are allowed in pleasure grounds, picnic areas, riverside swan trail.

TATTERSHALL CASTLE

Tattershall Castle, Tattershall, Lincoln, LN4 4LR.
(0526) 342543

Ownership: The National Trust.

Status: The National Trust.

General Description: The Castle, built about 1440 by Ralph,
Lord Cromwell, Treasurer of England under Henry VI,
consists of five levels and a battlement walkway, 100 feet
high from where spectacular views can be obtained. The
intermediate floors each contain small rooms in the corner
turrets and a single enormous state room complete with
magnificent carved stone fireplaces. The second floor has
been partly furnished with tapestries and oak furniture.
Surrounding the Castle is a double moat, home to ducks and
other water fowl. Peacocks strut across the lawns. There is a
small museum in the Old Guardhouse.

Open: April to October, every day, 10.30 a.m. – 5.30 p.m.
November to March, every day (except Christmas Day and
Boxing Day), 12 noon – 4.00 p.m.

Admission: Adults: £1.90; Children: 90p; Reductions for pre-
booked parties of fifteen or more.

Facilities: Car park (free to visitors), shop, museum, toilets.

Disabled Access: Shop, grounds and ground floor of Castle
accessible for wheelchair users, special toilet.

Additional Information: Picnics welcome in grounds, dogs
in car park only (on leads).

TINTAGEL CASTLE

Tintagel, Cornwall, PL34 0AA.
(0840) 770328

Ownership: English Heritage.

General Description: The setting of Tintagel Castle is
spectacular, on the wild and windswept Cornish coast, remote
and isolated on a small island linked to the mainland by a
narrow isthmus. Remains are strewn all over the island. Paths
lead to the shingle beach below and the large cavern known
as Merlin's Cave. The legend of King Arthur at Tintagel is an
enigma which has baffled historians and archaeologists alike
for many years, but gradually the island is yielding the secrets
of its past. Seeing Tintagel properly involves a certain
amount of climbing up and down steep steps which are
slippery in wet weather, so come prepared. Work to discover
the secrets of Tintagel's past is still being carried out. There is
still much to learn, and the mystery is not yet solved. On
sunny days the archaeologists continue their excavations, but
when the mists come swirling through Merlin's Cave and the
surf thunders against the cliffs, the mind turns to ancient
folklore and myths – the true history of Tintagel is still
hidden in the dim and distant past.

Open: Good Friday or 1st April (whichever is earlier) to 30th
September, open daily, 10 a.m. – 6 p.m. 1st October to
Maundy Thursday or 31st March, open every day 10 a.m. –
4 p.m.

Admission: Adults: £1.60; Senior Citizens, Students and UB40 Holders: £1.20; Children: 80p; special party rates.

Facilities: Car park in village ($^{1}/_{2}$ mile), toilets, gift shop, refreshments nearby, small exhibition.

TIVERTON CASTLE

Tiverton, Devon, EX16 6RP.
(0884) 253200

Ownership: Mr. and Mrs. A. K. Gordon.

Status: Private ownership.

General Description: Tiverton has a fascinating history spanning nearly 900 years. Originally built as a royal fortress by Richard de Redvers by command of Henry I in 1106, it passed by inheritance to the powerful Courtenay Earls of Devon, one of whom married Princess Katherine Plantagenet, daughter of Edward IV. During the Civil War the Castle was besieged by Fairfax in October 1645, and fell due to a lucky shot to a drawbridge chain. Shortly afterwards part of the fortifications were demolished, and the Castle became a peaceful private house. Still to be seen are a fine medieval gatehouse and tower (with garderobe), romantic ruins of solar and curtain walls, and entrance to secret passages, now impassable. The Castle contains an important Civil War armoury, some pieces of armour can be tried on by visitors, a panel of the New World Tapestry to which visitors are encouraged to add their stitches in history, and a notable clock collection.

Open: Good Friday to last Sunday in September, Sundays to Thursdays, 2.30 p.m. – 5.30 p.m. Open at other times to parties of more than twelve by appointment.

Admission: Adults: £2.50; Children to 7 free; 7-17: £1.50.

Facilities: Free parking inside for visitors, tea rooms open July and August, small souvenir shop.

Disabled Access: Ground floor and gardens accessible, half-price admission, ground floor toilet but no rail.

Additional Information: Dogs on leads in grounds.

TONBRIDGE CASTLE

Castle Street, Tonbridge, Kent, TN9 1BG.
(0732) 770929

Ownership: Tonbridge and Malling Borough Council.

Status: Local Authority.

General Description: In a beautiful setting by the River Medway, the motte and bailey castle site at Tonbridge is full of historical interest. New for Spring 1992 a re-creation of medieval life in the thirteenth century Castle Gatehouse, as it was over 700 years ago. Enjoy an atmospheric audio walk through the delightful grounds. Tour available in English Historical and Rhyme. Induction loops are also available for the Hard of Hearing. Situated on the A26 just off Tonbridge High Street.

Open: Easter to end September, Monday to Saturday, 9 a.m. – 5 p.m. Sunday and Bank Holidays, 10.30 a.m. – 5 p.m. October to end March, Monday to Friday, 9 a.m. – 5 p.m. Saturday, 9 a.m. – 4 p.m., Sunday, 10.30 a.m. – 4 p.m. Closed Christmas & New Year (last tour 1 hour before closing time).

Admission: Adults: £2; All concessions: £1; Groups: One person free with every ten.

Facilities: Pay and display parking, coach park at Tonbridge Farm off A227, refreshments at open air pool nearby May to September, five minutes walk into town for large selection, audio visual show included in Gatehouse Attraction.

Disabled Access: Limited access to suite and only ground floor of Gatehouse. Site is ancient monument and we have been unable to make alterations for lift access etc.

Additional Information: Picnics in grounds, dogs on lead, swimming, pitch and putt, tennis nearby.

TOTNES CASTLE

Castle Street, Totnes, Devon, TQ9 5NU.
(0803) 864406

Ownership: English Heritage.

Status: English Heritage.

General Description: A superb motte and bailey castle, with splendid views across the roof tops and down to the river. A fine example of a Norman fortification that never saw the heat of battle disturb its surroundings.

Open: Good Friday/1st April (whichever earlier) to 30th September, daily, 10 a.m. – 1 p.m., 2 p.m. – 6 p.m. 1st October to Maundy Thursday/31st March, Tuesday to Sunday, 10 a.m. – 1 p.m., 2 p.m. – 4 p.m.

Admission: Adults: 95p; Concessions (Students, UB40, over 60's): 75p; Children under 16: 45p; Children under 5, English Heritage members and pre-booked educational visits free.

Facilities: Very small shop at castle, parking in town (70 yards), refreshments and toilets in town (100 – 150 yards).

Disabled Access: Limited, most of castle up 70 steps.

Additional Information: Dogs allowed on a lead, good place for a picnic although no tables provided.

TOWER OF LONDON

Tower Hill, London, EC3N 4AB.
(071) 709 0765

Ownership: Managed by Secretary of State for the
Environment on behalf of Her Majesty The Queen.

Status: Historic Royal Palaces Agency.

General Description: The Tower of London is one of the
best preserved and most famous fortified buildings in the
world. Begun in 1078 by William the Conqueror, in its 900-
year history the Tower has been a palace, prison, treasury,
arsenal, mint, and even a zoo! Today the Tower houses the
fabulous Crown Jewels, and the Royal Armouries'
magnificent collections of arms and armour which date back
to Henry VIII. Also on view are the Instruments of Torture
and Punishment, the infamous Bloody Tower, and the
inscriptions by many famous and unknown prisoners in the
Beauchamp Tower. The Wall Walk takes visitors around the
Tower's ramparts, offering some fascinating glimpses of
history along the way. Free guided tours are given by the
famous Yeoman Warders and, of course, the Tower is home
to the legendary Ravens.

Open: March to October, Monday to Saturday, 9.30 a.m. –
6 p.m., Sunday 2 p.m. – 6 p.m. (last ticket sold 5 p.m.);
November to February, Monday to Saturday, 9.30 a.m. –
5 p.m. (last ticket sold 4 p.m.). Closed Sundays, closed 1st
January, Good Friday, 24th to 26th December.

Admission: Adult: £6.; Child (age 5 ÷ 15): £3.70; Senior Citizens/UB40/Student: £4.50; Disabled: £4.50 (paying disabled visitor can bring one adult helper free); Family Ticket: £17 (admits 5 – not more than 2 adults). 10% discount for groups of eleven or more.

Facilities: Parking – none on site, car and coach parking nearby in Lower Thames Street, drop off and pick up possible on Tower Hill (Main Entrance), cafeteria on wharf between Tower and River Thames.

Disabled Access: Due to age and design of buildings, disabled access is very limited. Wheelchair users not allowed in Lower Vault of Jewel House (Crown Jewels display). Disabled toilet facilities, wheelchairs available for loan, paying disabled visitors allowed to bring one helper free of charge.

Additional Information: Picnic area at wharf cafeteria, only guide dogs are allowed. Free Yeoman Warder guided tours.

Upnor Castle

High Street, Upnor, Rochester, Kent, ME2 4XG.
(0634) 718742

Status: English Heritage.

General Description: This well preserved sixteenth-century Gun Fort was built to protect Queen Elizabeth I's warships. However in 1667 it failed to prevent the Dutch Navy which stormed up the medway destroying half the English fleet.

Open: 1st April to 30th September, open daily, 10 a.m. – 6 p.m.

Admission: Adults: £1.50; Senior Citizens, Unemployed and Students: £1.10; Children: 75p.

Facilities: Parking (at a slight distance from Castle – Park before village).

Disabled Access: Grounds only.

Additional Information: Dogs only allowed in certain areas.

WALMER CASTLE

Kingsdown Road, Deal, Kent, CT14 7LJ.
(0304) 364288

Ownership: English Heritage.

Status: English Heritage.

General Description: Official residence of the Lords Warden of the Cinque Ports from early years of eighteenth century. Including William Pitt, Lord Livopool, the Duke of Wellington. Present Lord Warden is H.M.the Queen Mother. Inside the Castle are furnished rooms used by the Lords Warden plus the original Wellington Boots. Rooms used by Queen Victoria and Albert during their visit in 1842. Fine examples of mid-eighteenth-century furniture. Includes large gardens laid out by William Pitt's niece, Lady Nester Stanhope.

Open: 1st April or Good Friday (whichever is earlier) to 30th September, 10 a.m. – 6 p.m. daily. 1st October to1st April or Good Friday, 10 a.m. – 4 p.m. Closed Mondays. Closed January and February.

Admission: Adult: £2.50; Reduced Rate: £1.90; Children under 16: £1.30.

Facilities: Easy free parking, no refreshments, Soundaline tape tour free.

Disabled Access: Building contains stairs, wheelchairs access to ground floor and gardens.

Additional Information: Toilets available, picnics in grounds, no dogs.

WARKWORTH CASTLE

Warkworth, Near Amble, Morpeth, Northumberland, NE65 0UJ.
(0665) 711423

Status: English Heritage.

General Description: Originally a motte and bailey castle,
strengthened in the twelfth century by a stone curtain wall it
became a fitting stronghold for the Earls of Northumberland.
From the twelfth century it was steadily improved to the end
of the Middle Ages. The magnificent keep, built in the shape
of a Greek cross, dominates the castle and village. Like other
border castles, it suffered at the hands of both sides.
Shakespeare wrote of the conspiracy hatched at Warkworth
to dispose of Henry IV. James I of England and VI of
Scotland visited Warkworth in 1617. Visitors to the castle are
recommended to visit Warkworth Hermitage 1/2 mile
upstream from the castle, a fourteenth-century chapel, carved
inside the rock face. Only accessible by rowing boat at
summer weekends.

Open: Castle: 1st April to 30th September, daily, 10 a.m. –
6 p.m. 1st October to 31st March, Tuesday to Sunday,
10 a.m. – 4 p.m. Hermitage: 1st April to 30th September
weekends only.

Admission: Castle: Adult: £1.10; Reduced: 85p;
Children: 55p. Hermitage: Adult: 75p; Reduced: 55p;
Children: 40p.

Facilities: Parking at Castle (free), Audio Tours (Charge), toilets, small souvenir kiosk.

Disabled Access: Disabled access except to Keep, none at Hermitage.

Additional Information: Picnics allowed within castle, dogs on leads welcome, 15% reduction on groups of eleven and over, free educational visits.

WARWICK CASTLE

Warwick, Warwickshire, CV34 4QU.
(0926) 495421

Ownership: Warwick Castle Ltd., wholly owned subsidiary of the Tussauds Group.

Status: Privately owned.

General Description: Rising majestically from a sandstone bluff on the banks of the River Avon, Warwick Castle is set in over sixty acres of grounds landscaped by 'Capability' Brown. The interiors boast an impressive Armoury, gruesome Dungeons and Torture Chambers, and a haunted Ghost Tower. One can stroll through the Private Apartments amongst the wax figures of Madame Tussaud's award-winning exhibition 'A Royal Weekend Party 1898'. Countless art treasures are to be found throughout the Castle, but especially in the magnificent State Rooms and awesome Great Hall, with its gigantic Kenilworth Buffet, carved from a single Oak! Outside one can wander through the Woodland Garden and Victorian Rose Garden, or visit the eighteenth-century Conservatory housing the superb exact replica of the famous Warwick Vase. Breathtaking views of the rolling Warwickshire countryside can be seen from the mighty towers or the ancient mound, the oldest part of the Castle.

Open: November to February, open daily (except Christmas Day), 10 a.m. – 4.30 p.m. March to October, open daily, 10 a.m. – 5.30 p.m.

Admission: Individuals: Adult: £6.25; Child: £3.80; Senior Citizens: £4.25; Student: £4.75. Groups of twenty or more people: Adult: £5.00; Child: £3.25; Senior Citizens: £3.95; Student: £4.45. 2 Adults and 2 Children: £17.50; 2 Adults and 3 Children: £19.50.

Facilities: Parking, two restaurants (one self-service, one waitress service), refreshment kiosks, ice cream, cafe, nature trails.

Disabled Access: Disabled toilets and access to grounds, due to medieval features of castle, access to buildings strictly limited.

Additional Information: Dogs not permitted in grounds or castle, provision for picnics.

YARMOUTH CASTLE

Quay Street, Yarmouth, Isle of Wight, PO41 0PB.
(0983) 760678

Ownership: English Heritage.

Status: English Heritage.

General Description: Situated on one side of Yarmouth
Harbour, Yarmouth Castle was a late addition to Henry VIII's
coastal defences. Completed in 1547 and square in plan
instead of round, it possesses the earliest surviving arrowhead
bastion in England. It is surrounded by the sea on two sides
and once had a moat on the other two. In 1669 the Captain of
the island, Sir Robert Holmes, reduced the size of the castle
by filling in the moat, demolishing the earthworks, and
building a house, now a hotel, on the edge of the moat. There
are magnificent views of the Solent from the gun platform.
Exhibition of paintings 'Past and Present' by local artist
(Muriel Owen).

Open: 1st April to 30th September, 10 a.m. – 6 p.m., daily.
Closed 1 p.m. – 2 p.m. for lunch.

Admission: Adult: £1.50; Senior Citizens: £1.10; Students:
£1.10; UB40 Holders: £1.10; Children: 75p.

Facilities: Toilets situated nearby, parking is in public car
park about ¼ mile away.

Disabled Access: Access to ground floor only for wheelchair
users.

Additional Information: Dogs allowed.